John H. Balfour, John Macturk, Joseph H. Collins

Physical Geography

For Use in Science Classes and Higher and Middle Class Schools

John H. Balfour, John Macturk, Joseph H. Collins

Physical Geography
For Use in Science Classes and Higher and Middle Class Schools

ISBN/EAN: 9783337159030

Printed in Europe, USA, Canada, Australia, Japan

Cover: Foto ©Paul-Georg Meister /pixelio.de

More available books at **www.hansebooks.com**

J. Adams,
    Neam Hurst,
        Ambleside.

MR. PISISTRATUS BROWN, M.P.,

IN

THE HIGHLANDS.

"Is there a black Macintosh here?" asked the Guard.
"No, we are a' red MacGregors."

Page 4.

MR. PISISTRATUS BROWN, M.P.,

IN

THE HIGHLANDS.

Reprinted from "THE DAILY NEWS," *with Additions.*

LONDON:
BRADBURY, EVANS, AND CO., PRINTERS, WHITEFRIARS.

CONTENTS.

CHAPTER I.
THE FRITH OF CLYDE . . . . PAGE 1

CHAPTER II.
UP TOWARDS LOCH GOIL 14

CHAPTER III.
THROUGH HELL'S GLEN 24

CHAPTER IV.
DOWN LOCH FYNE 34

CHAPTER V.
THROUGH THE CRINAN 44

CHAPTER VI.
FROM CRINAN TO OBAN 56

CHAPTER VII.

OBAN 66

CHAPTER VIII.

FROM OBAN TO JURA 75

CHAPTER IX.

DEER-STALKING IN JURA 86

CHAPTER X.

DEER-DRIVING IN JURA 101

CHAPTER XI.

GROUSE-SHOOTING IN JURA 114

CHAPTER XII.

AMONG THE MOUNTAIN HARES 130

CHAPTER XIII.

MR. BROWN, M.P., AT A HIGHLAND WEDDING . 147

CHAPTER XIV.

HOMEWARD BOUND 161

CHAPTER XV.

THE LAST TURN 176

MR. PISISTRATUS BROWN, M.P., IN THE HIGHLANDS.

CHAPTER I.

THE FRITH OF CLYDE.

Mr. Pisistratus Brown, M.P., started for the Highlands without any purpose or plan. It was my good fortune to meet him one morning, by the merest accident, in Princes Street, Edinburgh, where he stood on the pavement pensively looking up at the Scott Monument. Even at a distance, I had recognized the plump and comfortable figure of my friend of old, despite the fact that he was now clothed in a suit of grey tartan, with a Glengarry cap set coquettishly on his head. As I drew near, I could perceive that he was little altered—that the old familiar expression was there, which used to puzzle the Conservative benches, and attract the eyes of the reporters from their gallery above. For Mr. Disraeli is not the only member of the House of Commons whom popular imagination has gifted with a "Sphinx-like look." Mr. Brown, M.P., has it too. Nature intended the Member for Bourton-in-the-Marsh to be a jolly, laughing, humorous, and fat little man; but ever after Mr. Brown got into the House, it was observed that a certain gravity lay over his features. He had covered his jocular good-humour with a thin veil of care and thought. He had also caught a trick of passing his hand slowly over his brow, and up towards his shining bald head, as if there was that within which passed the outward show of his round face, and merry, clear, blue eyes. Sometimes, indeed, he was found to have his gaze fixed meditatively on the horizon, as if he were resolving within himself the finances of far Cathay, or planning some diplomatic manœuvre in the Khanats, to stem the slow-working stream of Russian aggression.

I asked him how he came to be in Edinburgh while the Houses of Parliament were still sitting. He passed his arm within mine, and said he would tell me.

"You know," said he, "the Liberal majority is already big enough! What is the use of my remaining in the House to be a mere voting unit? I have stolen away a week or two before the recess in order to do some work which will really be of benefit. I have brought with me a bundle of papers, documents, and letters, bearing on the gross grievances sustained by Her Majesty's Clerks of Customs, as regards salary and term of service; and I humbly think I cannot be better employed than in studying this important question."

I told Mr. Brown that he was quite right; that it was always better to work in the open air, when that was possible; and then we fell to talking of his projected tour through the Highlands.

It turned out, as I have said, that Mr. Brown, M.P., had no plan; but was not a member of the Imperial Legislature of Great Britain and Ireland certain to have plenty of invitations? In a few days' time his brethren of both Houses would be coming north; and there would be given him such opportunities of yachting, fishing, red-deer stalking, and grouse-shooting, as seldom fall to the lot of mortals. In the meantime he was free to lounge about, and study at his leisure the grievances of the Customs Clerks. I proposed that he should spend a few days in the Western Highlands, before going north. He consented, on condition that I should accompany him. That night we went through to Glasgow, and next morning started by train for Greenock, a beautiful day heralding our setting out.

"Is there a black Macintosh here?" asked the guard, popping his head into the carriage as we were in the bustle of getting out at Greenock.

"No, we are a' red MacGregors," was the reply.

This was the last joke we heard from the gay party of artists who had accompanied us from Glasgow—a handful of dare-devil youths, who had smoked, and laughed, and told stories about the "Paisley bodies," and even painted my companion's portrait inside the crown of his hat during the brief ride down from the commercial capital of Scotland. And so we stood upon the quay of Greenock, with all the world before us. In which of all these puffing and roaring steamers should we embark? Far out before us stretched the lake-like Frith of the Clyde—with a brisk breeze from the west curling up its clear waters, with the hills of Roseneath and Cowal lying in a faint haze of heat, with sea-gulls circling overhead, and out on the broad green waters innumerable white-sailed yachts that dipped to the waves as they steered their various courses towards the mouths of the lochs. All around the base of these distant hills we could see the tiny villages—white and shining in the sun—which are beloved of the Glasgow folks; nestlings of little stone villas built among the rocks and the trees, and fronting such spacious views and such lovely scenery as belong to no river in Europe. Should we dart up the Gare Loch and see the wonders of Glen Fruin? Or sail up the noble Loch Long to the rainy regions of Arrochar and the silent sides of Ben Ima? Or dive into Hell's Glen, and cross over to see the preparations being made for the Royal visit at Inverary Castle? Or linger about the Kyles of Bute, and forget the roar of the Metropolis and the strife of Parliament in the loneliness of the lovely Loch Striven? Amid the crowd of excited porters, and frantic mothers with wandering families, and irate fathers who had lost their fishing-rods, and amid all the hurry, and roar, and distraction of whistling pipes, and churning paddles, and clanging bells, it was impossible to arrive at a calm decision. And so we "took that which lay nearest us," and crossed the gangway, on chance, into a vessel bound for some unknown destination.

And, lo! as we stood out towards the open Frith, all the wild noise died down, and the prevailing sound was the monotonous throbbing of the paddles on the calm water. Greenock herself, probably the dirtiest town in this unhappy world, began to shimmer behind a gauzy veil of sunlight; while down by Gourock, towards the point at which the Cloch Lighthouse, white as a star, juts out into the blue sea, the low-lying line of hills grew faint and visionary. The other side of the estuary was gradually becoming more distinct; and along the western side of the promontory of Roseneath (which Sir Walter Scott in the story of Jeanie Deans mistakenly describes as an island) we came in sight of the imposing villas, and keeps, and castles, which the Glasgow merchants and shipbuilders have built over the sea there, perching them on plateaux of mica schist, and having them well surrounded by birch, and elm, and rowan. A village consisting of these cottages and castles, with plenty of wood around, and a picturesque shore in front, is a wondrous novelty to him who has derived his notions of the seaside from the monotonous sands and chalk-cliffs of the South of England. Mr. Brown can find no words—not even Parliamentary phrases—to express his profound surprise and delight with this sort of watering-place.

"Why," he says, "they'd call those mountains in my part of the country; and there seem to be lakes by the dozen that could swallow Grasmere and Windermere, and never wink over it; and every man seems to have dotted down his house wherever he liked on the side of the hills. Then the rocky shore, with its shingle; and the clear sea-water; and the clumps of forest stretching down to the sea—why is this not known?"

Mr. Brown, M.P., is a good deal more familiar with the sloping shores of Como, and the malodorous hotel at the foot of the Thuner See, and the gay boats on the Lake of Luzern, than with the meres and lochs of his native land; and in that respect he represents a much larger constituency than Bourton-in-the-Marsh. However, we steam into Kilcreggan and touch at Cove, and then cross over to the Holy Loch, and to the small village of Strone. At this point, which juts out into the Frith, and commands a magnificent view southward, with the misty peaks of Arran forming the furthest sign of land, Brown puts down his foot.

"You shall whisk me no further," he remarks. "I mean to study this section of Paradise before we continue our travels. For who knows but that we may suddenly find ourselves at the gates?"

I am anxious to advertise the Argyle Hotel at Strone. It is small and cleanly, and homely and comfortable; and as for its prices, they were so insignificant that we cannot now recall them. Strone itself is not a bustling place; and when Mr. Brown, M.P., came out to the steps of the inn, he seemed to reflect for a moment as to the chances of his settling down here to his great project.

"This is the very place," he remarked confidentially, "to spend a week in, and get up some subject. You know I have all those papers about the salaries of Customs clerks in my bag. Would you believe it, a member of the Ministry spent the whole of his holidays, a year or two ago, in going into this very matter. And it only needs the mastery of certain details to prove the excessive hardship——"

Mr. Brown never finished the sentence. His eye somehow got lost in the far distance where ships were crossing the broad blue plain lying between the Cloch Lighthouse and Dunoon. He forgot all about Parliament. How could one remember the dusky chamber, and the rows of orange faces, in view of this great breadth of sea, where the specks of steamers were slowly moving, with a line of smoke in their wake, and in view of the pleasant stretch of beach, where the clear green water was plashing idly on the pebbles? Up the Holy Loch, at the mouth of which Strone stands, the water lay still and blue as a sapphire, but out towards the sea there was a windy greyness that lost itself in the haze about Cumbrae and Bute. For some considerable time the contemplative member stood on the steps of the inn, as dead as the Sphynx to all outward impressions; and then, slowly coming back to the world around him, he found himself scanning an announcement which was posted up on a board at the end of the pier. It informed us that Mr. M‘Farlane was disposed to let out horses and carriages for hire. In a very few minutes thereafter we were seated in a waggonette, and on the way to Loch Eck and Ardentinny.

Very pleasant indeed is the shady drive under the great hills that lie above the Holy Loch; and where in all Westmoreland is there anything to compare with the amphitheatre of mountains, beneath which the loch narrows to a point, and loses itself amid the rushes that surround the mouth of the Echaig? Of course, if we were at Derwentwater or Rydal, we should point the finger of scorn at all Scotch hills and lakes—such being the natural consistency of the traveller. But what seemed to impress my companion most—especially as we got up the valley of the Echaig, and found the fresh-water Loch Eck stretching out before us under its splendid panorama of mountains—was the exceeding solitariness of the place. Here were no fashionable hotels or parties of elderly ladies being driven about in closed carriages, or villas built on the site of cottages once inhabited by poets. By the side of the lonely lake we came to a rude little inn where the Member for Bourton-in-the-Marsh and our Highland driver hob-and-nobbed over a trifle of honest Lagavulin whisky that had a look of peat-reek and moss-water about its soft yellow hue; and then, with freshened spirits and keener pace we dashed down the great and open glen that leads under the slopes of Cruachan back to Loch Long. How the long blue lake shone in the light as we came near it! and how green the trees were all about Ardentinny, where Tannahill met the lass whose praises are now sung in every Scotch village! Here too Mr. Brown, M.P., lingered awhile, remarking that a cautious man never pronounced upon whisky until he had tasted it twice. I think he said something about Sir Wilfrid Lawson—but that is not to the purpose. Suffice it to add that we drove back to Strone, along the level shores of Loch Long, in the calm of the evening; and there were plover whistling afar off in the twilight, and fish leaping up with a splash in the quiet bays.

Then, having returned to the Holy Loch, Mr. Brown would have dinner postponed for yet another couple of hours; and we went to enjoy the humble sport of deep-sea fishing. No man ever died from excitement over this form of amusement; but still, in the gathering darkness, with the mountains around the head of the loch growing of a deep purple under the clear silver-grey of the twilight, it had its recompenses. And by the time we hauled up anchor to row home, the lights of Strone were burning like stars of gold; and in the east there were a faint star or two; and high over the Cloch Lighthouse—which was sending a calm yellow ray over the sea—there rose the faint sickle of the moon, to touch the wet blades of our oars as they rose and fell.

CHAPTER II.

UP TOWARDS LOCH GOIL.

WITH the morning breeze blowing coolly in from the sea, through an open window that showed us the blue waters of the Frith, with the whiting and codlings he had caught the night before now lying crisp and hot on the table before him, with his eye ranging over fresh cream, and excellent butter, and hot rolls, Mr. Brown, M.P., would have been happy enough; but you may guess his frame of mind when a letter brought us both an urgent invitation to join the party on board the schooner-yacht Kittiwake, then lying up in Loch Shira, at the head of Loch Fyne. Now the owner of the Kittiwake is also an M.P.; but he sits on the Opposition benches, and during the session just closing has done his best to vex the Government. I remind the Member for Bourton-in-the-Marsh of this fact, and hint that he may as well be cautious about joining the Kittiwake.

"Mr. Gladstone won't see me," he replies, with a solemn wink, and in the half-whisper with which a boy talks of playing truant. "Besides, could you get any place more fitted than a yacht for beginning to study an off-subject seriously? Those Customs Clerks' salaries, you know——"

Some half-hour thereafter two contemplative travellers might have been seen on the small wooden pier of Blairmore, patiently waiting for the *Carrick Castle*. Blairmore is a place of excessive importance, for it has a telegraphic office; and it is a pretty place withal, its straggling row of cottages lying at the foot of what we English folks would call a mountain, while the bold rocks that form its shore alternate with charming little bays, where the clear wavelets plash on white sand and beds of pebbles. Its inhabitants, at this moment, apparently consist of three men, who sit on the rocks and bask idly in the sun; but as the *Carrick Castle* comes churning her way over from Kilcreggan, other signs of life become visible. Some young ladies who have been transacting business in the grocery store come down to the quay in full holiday-costume; and Mr. Brown—but there is no saying who may read this veracious narrative. Suffice it to say that the *Carrick Castle* at last arrives, with a prodigious blowing of steam and noise of paddle; that we scramble on board by a gangway which is almost perpendicular; and that, as we leave the quay to steam up the calm and lovely waters of Loch Long, my companion expresses his profound disgust to find, by recognising certain southern accents, that he has run against a batch of the inevitable tourists. Though why one tourist should hate all other tourists, and cherish wicked hopes that they may be drowned, or run over, or smashed up in a collision; and why any one traveller, abroad or at home, should think that all Europe was meant only for him, and draw a miraculous distinction between himself and the herd, is a problem which the British Association would fail to solve.

Once more we pass the half-dozen cottages that form the pretty village of Ardentinny, and then before us open out the northern stretches of Loch Long, with vast ranges of mountains rising beyond into the pale blue sky. Nowhere, perhaps, in all the West Highlands is there to be found so much variety of mountain outline as in this splendid group of hills—some of them low, and smooth, and undulating, with their patches of bracken and heather become as soft as velvet under the warm midday light—others more lofty, but still round and flowing in outline, with immense fir-forests stretching to their summit, and woolly fragments of cloud clinging here and there to the trees—and beyond these again serrated peaks, as blue and sharp as the outline of Arran when the island grows dark before a storm. To-day we have every variety of effect, as there are huge masses of white cloud slowly drifting over from the western sea; and now it is the knobbly heights of "Argyll's Bowling-green," and now it is the peaks of the Cobbler and Ben Ima, and again the far hills that stretch over to Loch Lomond that catch the dark blue shadows and brighten up again as the clouds pass.

That mountainous promontory which has been grimly called "Argyll's Bowling-green," cuts the upper portion of Loch Long into two branches; and the more picturesque of these two, Loch Goil, runs up between the hills for a matter of eight or ten miles. In summer-time nothing could be more still and beautiful than this little loch, when the woods, and crags, and mountains on both sides of it are reflected in its dark-blue mirror; but in winter-time storms rage in this tea-cup sufficient to account for its title of "the black Loch Goil." If this is the Loch Goil that swallowed up Lord Ullin's daughter and her lover, it must have been in the dead of winter that the Chief of Ulva's Isle stole away his bride from her angry father. There is another Loch Goil in Scotland, it is true; but popular will has assigned the scene of Campbell's tragic ballad to the deep and twisted lake that, in summer at least, lies placidly under the mighty shadows of Ben-an-Cruach and Ben Bheulah.

On a rock that juts out into the loch stand the shattered ruins of Carrick Castle (after which our bright little steamer is named), a building which must have proved a powerful stronghold in the old days when rapine and slaughter devastated those silent glens at the bidding of rival chiefs. But these Highland solitudes are fast becoming peopled —in the summer-time, at least—by the pushing and industrious Saxon, who saves up his money in Glasgow, and then comes down here to build a cottage, or a villa, or a castle—as his means and tastes suggest—at the foot of the mountains. The Gaelic-speaking population have become shepherds, fishermen, boatmen, and so forth; while there are in every village a number of inhabitants who have no ostensible occupation, but eke out a living by doing odd jobs in gardening or gamekeeping for the Lowland or English visitor. Yet these Highland folks retain many of the traditional characteristics of their race. They are hospitable, courteous, and quick in apprehension; while even the poorest of them have a certain self-respect and independence which is very different from certain peculiarities of our agricultural labourer. Ask a shepherd to show you the way if you happen to get lost among the hills, and he will walk a couple of miles to do so; he will accept a glass of whisky gravely, and sit down with you to converse about matters in general, and especially about a son of the Duke having married a daughter of the Queen; but in a few minutes he will have convinced the stranger that it would be impossible to offer him a shilling. But this independence and sense of equality—which is no assumption, but the natural habit of men who are unaccustomed to the social distinctions of cities—gets sadly impaired along the route that tourists, and, above all, English tourists, frequent. There the Highlander not unfrequently becomes a sort of Red Indian—greedy, cunning, obsequious, and given to copious drinking. Taking the bad with the good, however, the Highlanders are a fine race; and some—among them, I should think, Mr. Matthew Arnold—will regret that those Celtic tribes are being from day to day pushed farther back into the mountains, instead of holding their own and tempering Saxon civilization with their non-commercial virtues and their poetic and imaginative habit of mind.

When we landed at the little village of Lochgoilhead, and walked along the curve of the shore to Miss Baird's Inn, Mr. Brown once more put down his foot. He would not budge—Kittiwake or no Kittiwake.

"Who knows when I may be here again?" he asked (for it is said he has some dark notion of being appointed the governor of an unpronounceable island in the Pacific), "and do you think I am going to leave a spot like this without seeing it, merely because a man offers me a berth in a yacht? Besides, I *must* put those papers in order before going on board, you know——"

Mr. Brown did not touch the papers. Some

half-hour after luncheon, when he had sat and gazed down the loch, and admired the shadows of the mountains and clouds that mingled with the green rushes at the head of the lake, the spirit of the mountaineer arose in him, and nothing would do but an ascent of the highest hill in the neighbourhood. Accordingly we set out for the summit of Ben Donich, following for a time the course of a small river that comes tumbling in white and brown masses down a rocky channel. It was a tedious and laborious ascent, but when, after two hours' constant climbing, we stood by the heap of stones on the bare and windy top, the view amply repaid us. All around lay a magnificent panorama of mountains—on the north especially, they seemed to be huddled against each other like mighty waves that had been suddenly petrified; while far away in the south lay the broad waters of the Frith and the open sea, with a network of lochs, and islands, and promontories between. We sat there so long and so silent that a mountain-hare came out from its hiding, and then, catching sight of us, darted like lightning over the scant grass and the rocks. As we turned to descend, the hills west of Loch Fyne were growing purple under a pale yellow sunset; and Loch Goil, beneath our feet, lay still and grey under the dark shadows of Ben Bheulah and Ben-an-Lochan. Indeed, when we got down to the village, night had fallen; but it was the clear, pale-green night that in those high latitudes is only a twilight. We sate down to dinner when most of the inhabitants of Lochgoilhead had doubtless got to bed; and thereafter we discussed, over a small beaker of the wine of the country, our plans for the morrow.

"The coach that goes through Hell's Glen to Loch Fyne does not start till one o'clock," remarked the Member for Bourton-in-the-Marsh, "and before then I shall have time to take a look at those comparative scales of salaries."

CHAPTER III.

THROUGH HELL'S GLEN.

A WILD morning of rain, and wind, and driving mist had broken over Loch Goil and its amphitheatre of hills; and when Mr. Brown, M.P., looked out of his bedroom window he scarcely recognised the place. The loch was a plain of stormy grey, with white-tipped waves rushing up; Carrick Castle had disappeared as completely as if the Athol men had finished their work and swept it into the sea; while the great clouds of mist that came over from the west worked such wonders with the hills, that Ben Bheulah and Ben-an-Lochan seemed playing at hide-and-seek behind the vast white veil. But as the morning wore on a brief glimmer of sunshine broke out between the showers; and at length, while the clouds seemed to gather themselves up in black and thunderous masses over the entrance to Hell's Glen, a great splatch of blue appeared in the sky, and corresponding dashes of colour began to show on the lake. And then, across the bars of sunshine, the steamer came slowly up the loch; and as the noise of the funnel broke on the silence of the place, we made our way down towards the pier to catch one of the two coaches.

Behold us now perched on the box-seat of a huge vehicle, that has a team of five horses to draw it up and over the mountain-pass that lies between Lochgoilhead and Loch Fyne. Whether this gorge was called Hell's Glen by reason of the wild and rugged nature of its scenery, or on account of the intense heat that the mountains reflect down into its depths, it is hard to say; but at all events the whole place is haunted with legends of Satan, and a surly old gentleman who used to live in a solitary farm here came to be known as the devil himself. Shortly after leaving Lochgoilhead the road through the pass begins to ascend, and leads by the side of a rocky ravine, down which a powerful stream thunders night and day. In front of us the mountains seem to form a gigantic barrier, but gradually we catch a glimpse of a white road far up the side of a distant hill; and as the horses seem to have plenty to do, the road being rather heavy, we all get out and set out to climb up a short cut—a wet and slippery footpath, which leads through tangled oak, and willow, and birch. Away on the right of us glimmers the road that leads to Glencroe and that "Rest-and-be-thankful," on which Wordsworth wrote a sonnet and Lord Russell built up an oratorical illustration. Higher and still higher rises the road—while we occasionally overtake and occasionally lag behind, the painfully toiling coach; while the mountains in front are continually changing their aspect under the breezy sky. And at last, when we have nearly got to the end of the giant pass—the road on which we stand being itself 2,400 feet above the level of the sea—lo! at our feet we suddenly find the whole length of Loch Fyne, with its wooded hills shimmering greenly in the sun, and the small steamer at St. Catherine's waiting to take us across. We are still a few miles from the loch; but up on this height the broad shoulders of wild moorland that slope down to the water are as nothing; and we feel ourselves already opposite Inverary, and the grey castle of the Duke, that seems but a speck among the trees, and the bold front of Duniquoich, with its watch-tower perched high on the bare rock.

The descent from this pinnacle to St. Catherine's will never be forgotten by anyone who has sat on the box-seat of the coach. To drive a four-in-hand along Piccadilly and through the Park, and up again by Kensington-gore, seems to the uninitiated a comparatively safe and easy performance; but to take a team of five horses at full gallop down a steep mountain road, which has sharp turns in it, and an occasional narrow stone bridge that spans a chasm, is a very different matter. And as Mr. Brown felt himself getting through the air at an alarming rate of speed, he became silent. He had been talking Parliamentary rapture about the view; but now his face was fixed as that of Memnon, and he only turned his eyes from the necks of the five horses in front of him to the pile of trunks behind him, which threatened to come down and nip his head off as a girl might nip off a rosebud.

"Do you sometimes let a horse down?" he said at length, in a timid way, to the driver.

"Sometimes," was the grim reply.

"But, as a rule, they are sure-footed, eh?"

"Oo aye, as a rule; but a horse is no infallible, ony mair than a man."

Mr. Brown said nothing, but held firmly on, as the coach, and luggage, and passengers swung round the corners of bridges, or dipped into the hollows of the road. But when we finally got down to the shore, and stopped at St. Catherine's Mr. Brown descended, shook himself, and came forward with a very different look on his face. He was quite cheerful now. He spoke of the drive in a familiar and airy way, and asked if we had not " come a cracker" down that hill.

"I should not like to have brought those horses down," he said, critically scanning the team. "With a pair, you know, it would have been different."

Right opposite us now lay the straggling white houses of Inverary, and the handsome clumps of trees around the Duke of Argyll's castle, and the mouth of the little armlet of Loch Fyne that is known as Loch Shira.

"And there, as I live, is the Kittiwake coming over for us," remarked Mr. Brown, pointing to a handsome little cutter of about 30 tons that was running across the loch before a westerly breeze. I ventured to suggest to Mr. Brown—who is much more familiar with the forms of the House than with nautical matters—that schooner-yachts have, as a rule, two masts, and that this little cutter cannot fairly be suspected of measuring 60 tons.

"Ah, to be sure," said Mr. Brown carelessly. "I was thinking of something else—of those Customs clerks' papers, you know. I really forgot all about them this morning. But there will be plenty of time on board the yacht."

We crossed over Loch Fyne to Inverary in the little steamer that was waiting at the pier; and, as luck would have it, discovered the owner of the Kittiwake in the inn at which we begged for some lunch. The member for the ancient and historical borough of Slow, in Somersetshire, is a tall, bluff, rosy-cheeked gentleman, with a tremendous laugh, a fine belief in Conservative principles, and a knowledge of shooting and yachting which the editor of a sporting paper might envy. His name is Weyland, and he is the colonel of a Volunteer regiment. He is great in the House between half-past four and five; for he has the art of asking the Government the most vexatious conundrums, which no Minister can answer. We receive a boisterous and hearty welcome; and then says Mr. Brown—

"Wasn't it here that Dr. Johnson asked for a gill of whisky, to find out what made a Scotchman happy?"

The hint was enough; and the steward of the Kittiwake, who was in attendance, was ordered to bring in, for testing purposes, a jar of whisky that had just been purchased in the inn. Warmed with a moderate quantity of that fiery fluid, Mr. Brown's reminiscences came thickly on him.

"Didn't Captain Dalgetty visit this place? And there are herrings here, I know. And didn't Burns come to this very inn, or some other inn, and write on the window—

> Whoe'er he be that sojourns here,
>   I pity much his case,
> Unless he's come to wait upon
>   The lord their god his grace.
> There's nothing here but Hieland pride,
>   Hieland cauld and hunger:
> If Providence has sent me here,
>   'T was surely in his anger.

But what will the people say when the Queen comes? And—and—Weyland, old fellow, you're looking first rate."

Mr. Brown, indeed, was in excellent spirits as we started for a walk up to the castle that was then expected to receive a Royal visit. The building itself is not an architectural marvel—being a plain, square mass of grey chlorite-slate, with a tower at each corner, and a tall winged pavilion rising over the centre. But the position and surroundings of Inverary Castle are singularly beautiful. The rivers Aray and Shira brawl down from the mountains along rocky channels that come through dense woods, and are hanging with masses of ferns and wild flowers; the grounds around the castle are intersected by magnificent avenues of elms and limes, that have made many a fine perspective for the photograph; and the building itself, from the summit of a smooth plateau, faces the blue waters and steep hills of Loch Shira and Loch Fyne, and on the left, the bold peak of Duniquoich, that seems to keep guard over the far and unseen deer-haunts of Ardkinglas.

Thereafter we walked leisurely up and along the margin of Loch Shira, to the little bay in which the Kittiwake lay at anchor, her sails furled, and her graceful spars mirrored accurately on the still surface beneath. Mr. Brown was in such a gay humour, that he volunteered to steer the pinnace which was sent ashore for us; and the post of honour was willingly accorded to him. It seemed to one, at least, of the party whom he thus conducted, that he made one or two preliminary pulls with the ropes, to see which way the boat's head would turn; but all the same, we got safely towards the neighbourhood of the yacht, and then our coxswain wisely allowed the men to get up to the gangway by the manipulation of the oars. A proud man he was as he stepped on the white deck and looked around him on the trim and bright vessel, on the calm bosom of the lake, and the fair scenery around. His arms were crossed as are those of Dan O'Connell in the lobby of the Reform Club; and he appeared ready to burst out with a noble quotation from Sir Walter Scott. It would have been the deepest cruelty to hint that the Customs clerks were wearying for that reform in their salaries which he had privately undertaken to secure.

CHAPTER IV.

DOWN LOCH FYNE.

WHEN on the following morning Mr. Pisistratus Brown, M.P., came up on deck, no words could convey his surprise and delight with the comforts and luxuries of the Kittiwake. The ingenious manner in which use had been made of every corner; the pretty decorations in the saloon; the excellence of the meats and drinks that Weyland's steward had placed before us for supper—all were matter of enthusiastic encomium; but the climax of his praise was reached in describing how he found an elegant little wash-hand basin and a veritable fresh-water pipe in his bedroom. Here a shout of laughter was heard, and the Member for Slow put his head above the companion-ladder.

"Well, whatever you may call it," said Mr.

Brown, with some natural irritation, "it is a bedroom. I don't care whether it's a hatchway, or a tarpaulin, or a jib-boom, so long as I get a comfortable night's rest in it."

However, Mr. Brown soon began to pick up nautical phrases, and he could scarcely be persuaded to go below for breakfast, so interested was he in seeing the men get the Kittiwake under weigh. Indeed, no one spent much time over that meal, for we were all anxious to have a final look at Inverary. And so, when we again went on deck, we found the large white sails of the Kittiwake bending over before a gentle breeze, and as we bore down the blue waters of Loch Fyne, Inverary, and the grey castle, and the noble avenues of trees went slowly past us in a moving panorama. The mountains up by the head of the loch were still dim and misty, and away towards the deer-forests of Ardkinglas grey swathes of cloud still hung about the hills; but round about us the sun-light was clear and warm, striking on the breezy blue of the lake, on the white stretch of shore, and on the woods that were still green and moist with the dews of the night.

"If I were the Duke of Argyll," said the Member for Bourton-in-the-Marsh, as he pensively regarded the beautiful picture formed by the semicircular head of the loch, with Inverary Castle nestling under the woods and hills, "do you think I'd spend night after night in that melancholy hall listening to toothless old gentlemen mumbling incoherent speeches that the country doesn't care twopence about——"

"I wish you'd speak with more respect of the House of Lords," said the Member for Slow warmly. "Whatever the country may think, mind you, these men are doing their best for it, when they might, if they chose, be fishing in Norway, or enjoying themselves on the Mediterranean, or skylarking among these lochs, just like you and me, who have no business here whatever."

"I have only to say," remarked Mr. Brown, with some suspicion of reserve and coldness in his manner, "that I am not neglecting my duties voluntarily. When I think of the Ministry and my fellow-members continually sitting up till three or four o'clock in the morning in this weather, I should be ashamed to find myself here if I had not definite instructions from my doctor."

Here the Conservative Member was rude enough to wink; and one of our party, a large and good-natured Glasgow bailie, broke into a horse-laugh.

"Besides," continued Mr. Brown, taking no heed of the interruption, "a private member may do more good to his country by taking a brief holiday in order to study a certain subject, than by merely remaining to form a unit in a 'mechanical' majority that is already big enough. I have at this moment downstairs—well, I suppose I must say 'below'— papers on a financial topic which deserves, and even demands, serious consideration. The salaries of Government officials form a subject which requires careful scrutiny; and how can you give it more time and attention than by taking a short holiday?"

"I suppose you've found out that some police-clerk has 12*s*. 6*d*. a year more than he should have," said the Member for Slow, with a prodigious grin; and then, putting aside the quarrel, he asked Mr. Brown whether he preferred the Campbeltown or the Islay distilleries. Mr. Brown replied in favour of Lagavulin; and the political discussion was adjourned "*sine die* until the afternoon."

As we opened out the successive bays and headlands formed by the undulating shores of Cowal, the full stretch of Loch Fyne came broadly into view, until far in the south we could see the bold line of rocky cliff that runs down from Tarbert to Skipness, and beyond that again the pale blue mountains of Arran, showing a jagged and faint outline against the sky. No plan of our cruise had been as yet accurately decided upon; and it was left for Mr. Brown to say whether we should go through the Crinan Canal and take a trip to Oban, or go for a preliminary run through the Kyles of Bute and thereafter round by Arran, Cantire, and Islay. He decided on the former, but insisted in the first place that we should have an opportunity of seeing one of the fleets of Loch Fyne fishing-boats setting out, which he had heard was a most picturesque sight. It was acccordingly arranged that we should anchor in Loch Gilp for that day, and not attempt to go through the Crinan until the following morning. So it happened that we got down to Ardrishaig, at the end of the Crinan Canal, about mid-day; and when the yacht had been properly moored we went ashore to see the Iona come in with her cargo of tourists bound for the North.

When the stately steamer at length showed her two red funnels coming round the point, Mr. Brown hastened down to the pier, apparently with the notion that he might meet some friend from the South. But when the small and hurrying crowd bustled out of the boat, and struggled through the swarm of bare-footed boys anxious to carry their luggage for them, they were found to be all strangers, and Mr. Brown regarded them as they walked up to the small steamer on the canal, with a look of profound compassion. Yet why should tourists be regarded as strange and unhappy beings, whom one should regard with sympathy? There was nothing mournful in the procession of people who carried their hand-bags, and top-coats, and umbrellas, and what not, and who seemed to regard the little steamer on the canal as a mere toy after their acquaintance with the spacious and handsome Iona. We saw the poor creatures off. Somehow they seemed to be away from home. They were going out into that wild western region where the Atlantic waves roll in among lonely islands; and we half feared they might never return to the South, or that they might experience rain or some other dire evil. As for ourselves, we were going through the Crinan, too; but we should be quite at home, and were certain to enjoy it.

A fine sight it was, that setting out of the herring fleet in the yellow afternoon, with the bronzed and varnished hulls of the boats shining like so many spots of brownish red on the calm blue of the lake. Here, too, were none of the tattered and pot-bellied fishermen of Brighton, living on occasional hauls of mackerel and occasional shillings got from visitors—but crews of lithe and stalwart men, big-boned and spare-fleshed, who plied the enormous oars with a swing and ease that told of splendid physiques, hard exercise, and tolerably good living. The wind had entirely gone down, and the various boats that left the harbour in straggling groups formed a strange sort of picturesque regatta, their oars scarcely troubling that still plain of blue. Here and there a brown sail hung half-mast high, just in case a slight breeze might be got at the mouth of the Bay; but each boat had its four enormous oars regularly rising and falling as they all drew away from us. And we could hear the laugh and jest come across the still water, as two of the boats would get within speaking distance; and now and again a verse of some shrill Gaelic song would float towards us, the notes of it keeping time to the oars. The further the boats drew out towards the broad bosom of the loch, the deeper grew their colour under the warm and level light of the sun, until many of them seemed like rose-coloured buoys placed far out on that smooth plain. And then, as they reached a line of darker water on the loch, we could see them one by one run up the broad brown sail to catch the light breeze. And while we still sat and wondered how they would spend the long and dark night, and what songs would be sung by the side of the stove, and whether rain would compel them to make the sail into a tent, and what sort of take they would bring home with them in the cold grey hours of the dawn, lo! the boats had disappeared as if by magic, and there was nothing before us but the far and desolate shores of Cowal.

We had a pleasant evening in the snug little saloon of the Kittiwake; and Mr. Brown for once postponed the consideration of the Customs clerks' grievance in order to stake sixpences at loo (limited). And then, as he departed to his stateroom (having won the price of a box of cigars, or thereabouts), he informed us that on the next day he would show us all how to detect the presence of water-hens.

"*Cras*, to-morrow, *iterabimus*, we sail, *ingens æquor*, through the Crinan Canal."

These were his parting words; and they were very fairly pronounced.

CHAPTER V.

THROUGH THE CRINAN.

WHAT is a canal? The ordinary answer would be, a narrow and monotonous channel filled with a yellow fluid, that connects disagreeable places, and is the medium of a cheap and unpicturesque traffic. The dull-hued snake that winds about our manufacturing towns, that lies amid coal-dust and the refuse of factories, is, if possible, a more hideous thing than the melancholy suburbs around it. But there are canals and canals; and up here in Argyleshire a canal becomes a succession of clear little lochs, connected by a line of artificial channel that runs through the most charming scenery, and has its banks laden with trees, and bushes, and tangled masses of wild flowers. Here the small Highlander angles with a bent pin for fish that he can see down in the cool, clear depths; here the water-hen hides in the sedges, or sails out on the calm surface to call her young together. As you walk along the grassy banks every hundred yards produces a new picture—from the moment you leave the blue sweep of Loch Gilp behind until you come in sight of Loch Crinan and the wild rocks that guard the harbour from the force of the western sea. On your right hand stretches a far plain, that is varied with stream, and wood, and rock; on your left the peaks of the Knapdale mountains are shut off by a range of hills that almost overshadow the canal, and are clad in all the verdure of bracken, and moss, and young oak and birch. You can hear the murmuring of streams in the deep little glens that are cloven in their side; and you can hear the call of the blackcock far up on the heathery knolls that shine in rosy purple under the fierce light of the midday sun. The small lakes that are strung like pearls on the lithe band of the canal are wonders of loveliness; and if you can only manage to escape the passage of the steamer you may forget that this is a canal, and find yourself lost in the utter loneliness of Highland scenery.

There is every facility, too, for the stranger to enjoy the walk from Loch Gilp to Loch Crinan; for towards the western side of the canal there are fifteen locks, and as the whole distance is only nine miles, one has ample time to get to Crinan on foot. Indeed, when we had seen the Kittiwake started on her voyage, we took no more thought of her, and speedily lost sight of her. Mr. Brown's parting with her was almost pathetic; he had acquired such a tenderness for the yacht as men get for favourite horses that have served them well.

"She looks like a queen taken captive," he said, as they began to drag her ignominiously along. "I suppose when we see her in Loch Crinan, she will have her sails up again and be something like herself—freshening herself up, as it were, for her northward flight. And we shall see Jura, shall we not?—and Scarba, and Corryvreckan, and Colonsay? I declare to you, all last night, as the yacht lay and rolled in the ripple of the bay, it seemed to keep time to that old ballad about the Chief of Colonsay. You know how it goes—

> As you pass through Jura's Sound.
> Bend your course by Scarba's shore,
> Shun, oh! shun the gulf profound,
> Where Corryvreckan's surges roar.

Wouldn't the house rise to a quotation like that—say that you were warning the Government against courting Opposition cheers"—and here the Member for Bourton-in-the-Marsh unconsciously paused; but his arm was still uplifted, and he gazed into blank space, as if his glittering eye had in reality seized the Treasury Bench and pinned Mr. Gladstone there.

We were fortunate enough to miss the swarm of bare-footed young Celts who haunt the passengers by the steamer, and offer to transact business in milk and hazel-nuts. We only met one of them—a small maiden of six or seven, with sun tanned arms and feet, and hair so prodigiously fair as to be almost white. It was at the Carnbaan Inn — a convenient resting-place at the beginning of the series of locks. Mr. Brown, obeying a maxim of his medical adviser—"Wherever you travel, the safest drink is the *vin du pays*"—had refreshed himself with a modest quantity of the Lagavulin he had grown to love, and was just coming out of the inn when that "kleine Marketenderin" came forward with a little tin jug in her hand, and said with the peculiar Highland inflexion that distinguishes North from South Scotland, "Are ye for any nits, sir?" Mr. Brown looked at the small and timid merchant, and said, "My little girl, I don't know what you say; but you are too pretty a little girl to have no shoes and stockings, and so you will take this half-sovereign to your mother and tell her to buy you some."

Remonstrance with Mr. Brown, M.P., about this preposterous action was of no avail. It was useless to point out to him that he was corrupting a hardy and independent population; that all over the Highlands the children enjoyed the freedom and health of running about with bare feet and legs; and that this small girl was being transformed from a merchant into a pauper. He folded up the coin in a piece of paper, and bade her put it in her pocket. Then in the most natural way in the world, she held out the jugful of hazel-nuts in return. The Member for Bourton-in-the-Marsh looked puzzled. He might have answered off-hand a conundrum about the Babs of Persia, or even accepted at a moment's notice the command of an iron-clad, but he could not for the life of him tell what to do with two handfuls of green nuts. Yet there was a principle at stake: he was forced to take them. Finally he bethought himself of his hat: and so it befell that, until we were well out of sight of that little Highland woman, a member of the Imperial Legislature of this country walked with a hatful of nuts in his hand, while an almost vertical sun was pouring down its fiercest rays on his bald head.

Weyland, M.P. for Slow, and two other members of our party, had gone on during this exciting adventure; and we eventually found them sitting in dead silence behind a group of tall bushes, opposite a part of the canal where there were abundant rushes on the other side. Weyland had in his hand a large black air-cane; the Glasgow bailie was regarding rather timorously a saloon pistol. Mr. Brown became quite excited.

"You just watch me bring a moor-hen out. I will undertake to bring a moor-hen out in ten minutes from these rushes, and as many water-rats as you like from the bank there—for half-a-sovereign I will."

"It is rather a mean way of making up your losses by generosity," I remark; and then Mr. Brown creeps up on tiptoe to the bushes. His finger is on his lips. He sits down with an awful air of compressed energy on his face; and then, in the stillness, he begins his performance. Since the days of Herr Von Joel—those happy days when songs, and glees, and choruses had not been supplanted by acrobats and ventriloquists—no man has imitated the call of a bird as Mr. Brown now succeeds in doing. It is marvellous. We almost feel ourselves becoming moor-hens under the process. Only the real moor-hens do not seem to appear. Through chinks in the leaves we scan the dense rushes; but there is no sign of that half-domestic wild fowl, whose yellow bill and bobbing head and white cleft tail are alike familiar to English rivers and to Scotch moorlands. But lo! as if by magic another bird bobs up in the middle of the water, some distance further down. "A dabchick!" is the mental exclamation of every one, and stealthily the smooth black tube that Weyland holds is pointed through the leaves. There is a sharp click, a splash in the water, and the next moment the dabchick is lying on the surface of the canal, its legs uppermost.

"You've spoilt your chance of getting a water-hen all for that miserable dabchick," said Mr. Brown, with some irritation.

"That miserable dabchick!" cried Weyland,

"You can take the breast of this dabchick, and give it to your lady-love to wear for your sake; but what could you do with a water-hen? Four-and twenty of them could hardly flavour a steak-pie; and then ketchup would do it as well."

"I should have had a moor-hen out in another minute," said Mr. Brown.

"Never mind," said the Opposition Member; "you can work the charm another time."

Mr. Brown soon recovered from his disappointment, and began to talk enthusiastically of all that we were to see and do when we had got out to the wilder islands in the west. He had vague plans for testing the flesh of various sea-fowl, to judge whether the home-produce of this country might not extend its area, and an addition be made to the food of the poor. Then he bethought him of making a collection of stuffed birds, all of his own killing, ranging from the lordly solan down to the sea-lark.

"We shall have abundance of time," he remarked confidentially, "once we have got rid of these obstructions; and you will see how I shall knock off that business connected with the grievances of the Customs clerks. I should be ashamed of having postponed the matter so long, but that the delay was unavoidable. How could one get up statistics, and make comparisons of tables, when we had all the bother of getting through the canal before us? Nobody would expect one to carry a bundle of papers nine miles, and sit down to work by the side of the road, could they? I don't think I neglect my duty any more than anybody else. I am sure I don't—I am the last man in the world to do so. But you've got to draw the line somewhere, and humour Nature, and temper mental work by physical exercise, or where would you be?"

Mr. Brown spoke in quite an appealing and almost injured tone, which was quite unnecessary. Anybody who knows the inhabitants of Bourton-in-the-Marsh is aware that not for worlds would they change their representative; and as for the

Customs clerks, they are so accustomed to waiting that they won't mind.

Towards the afternoon we were overtaken by the gaily-painted little screw steamer that transfers travellers going North from the Iona to the kindred vessel lying at Crinan. As we reached that small port, which nestles in a corner of a rocky bay, the great steamer had sailed away towards Oban, and the Kittiwake was lying out at anchor. When we had got on board, Mr. Brown went to the bow and surveyed the prospect. There was rather a lowering sky in the West; but the gloom only heightened the wild and vague look of the rocks and islands lying out in the western sea, with the dusky peaks of Jura lying down in the South. All manner of sea-birds were visible; from the familiar gull that circled overhead, to the lonely heron that stood out at some distant promontory, a grey shadow against the dark rock. Mr. Brown went below to rummage among Weyland's guns, and was disappointed to find that there were not over thirty or forty cartridges ready made. However, he came on deck again; and, in the fast-falling darkness, his talk was all of shooting-adventures, and storms, and rocks, and legends, and the delight of being separated from mankind. He was as anxious for the morrow as " the brave Macphail" who fell in with a mermaid as he was returning to his love of Colonsay; and Weyland, who had discovered his friend's copy of Leyden's poems, read out in noble accents these appropriate lines :—

> The lonely deck he paces o'er,
>   Impatient for the rising day;
> And still from Crinan's moonlight shore,
>   He turns his eyes to Colonsay.

CHAPTER VI.

FROM CRINAN TO OBAN.

As the tall Kittiwake stood out from Crinan Bay, with her white sails filled with a light breeze, her smooth decks shining in the sun, and her bows dipping gracefully to the long and even swell coming in from the Atlantic, Mr. Brown, M.P., clinging stoutly to the steel shrouds, became quite enthusiastic over the loveliness of the scene before him. He descanted to us on the wild and desolate look of Jura, with her gloomy mountains rising up in the southern sky; he turned to the smaller islands near him, and pointed out their rich colours that were soft and smooth in the haze of the heat; his eagle eye detected all manner of strange sea birds poised over or floating on the blue waters; and he declared that the motion of the yacht was delightful.

"Interfusa nitentes vites æquora Cycladas," he exclaimed, in quite a solemn and parliamentary tone,—"avoid the turbulent sea amid the shining Cyclades, as one might say; but did the Cyclades ever shine in bluer waters than these, and did Horace ever see islands more fair in his dreams of the Mediterranean? And I would dare to add that there is more imaginative power in the wild legends that hallow those lonely rocks and seas than in a cartload of the stories connected with the puddles and sand-hills of Greece. Homer! I maintain that there is more depth of passion, of emotion, and of strong human interest in such a ballad as 'Helen of Kirkconnel' than in twenty Iliads all boiled up together in a tin pot; and as for the blatant history of that nincompoop Æneas, it is as atrocious a piece of commonplace manufacture as was ever committed in this miserable world; and if you want true imaginative and lyrical power, which is the sum and substance of poetry——"

Mr. Weyland, from the companion-ladder, handed up a breech-loader. The Member for

Bourton-in-the-Marsh regarded it for a moment with contempt; but he took it, nevertheless, and began to place a couple of cartridges in the barrels. We heard no more of Mr. Brown's theories of poetry, for he carefully made his way up to the bow, and placed himself there so that he might have a shot at any of those wild creatures which he had ventured to name for us. It is remarkable, however, that with two members of Parliament on board no one could find out in what month the statutory prohibition of shooting sea-fowl ends; but then, as Mr. Weyland remarked, it would be a hard thing if people who made the laws were not allowed to break them.

And so the Kittiwake sped on, opening out the Dorus Mhor, or Great Gate, and gradually getting into those long swirls of sea that sweep round from Scarba, and produce strange bubblings and lines of foam on the calmest day. Away over on our left lay the channel between Jura and Scarba, where the whirlpool of Corryvreckan raves. We listened intently to catch the strange noise of its waters, which has been described by many a poet as for ever haunting " the distant isles that hear the loud Corbrechtan roar." Campbell, who lived some miles to the south of Loch Crinan, says that even there he could hear the sound of the Corryvreckan straits. " When the weather is calm, and the adjacent sea scarcely heard on these picturesque shores, its sound, which is like the sound of innumerable chariots, creates a magnificent and fine effect." No echo reached us of the turmoil which generally does prevail in that narrow channel. But all around us were evidences of those powerful currents that have gained for Corryvreckan its legendary fame. The sea around us seemed to boil up from mighty springs; and here and there, between those spacious circles of foam, we could see the thin hard line of a current. As the Kittiwake slowly made headway through the calm-looking whirlpools, her bow was caught every few minutes by some powerful stream, and twisted round with a sudden jerk. At other times she would come to a dead stop, as if she had run against a wall of iron. But so far from there being anything in the shape of a picturesque whirlpool, with a hollow centre, and a circumference of tossing waves, even the low ground swell of the Atlantic had disappeared. It is easy to understand, however, that these treacherous currents may, at certain seasons of the year, be greatly intensified in the rocky channel between Scarba and Jura; and, although the whirlpool of Corryvreckan, as it figures in books illustrative of natural wonders, is a myth, the swirls of the sea in the narrow straits have destroyed many a boat and drowned many a man, while in the calmest season the passage is never without a certain danger. Weyland, who is somewhat anxiously looking after the conduct of the Kittiwake, tells us that one evening last summer a profound excitement was caused in Oban by the report that the large steamer from Crinan, with all its valuable cargo of Southern tourists, had been drawn into the whirlpool of Corryvreckan, and wrecked on the rocks of Scarba. How such a wild story became current in a town which must be familiar with the channel, it is difficult to understand; but, as a matter of fact, hour after hour passed, and the steamer did not come in. Next morning, when everyone hurried down to the Quay to learn the news, the safety of the steamer was secured, but various forms of wild stories were being told of perilous escapes and dangers by sea. It eventually turned out that the mate of the steamer had sighted some smack or similar sailing vessel drifting towards Corryvreckan; that he, with a couple of men, put off in a boat and overtook her, found her a derelict, and towed, or endeavoured to tow, her back to the steamer, while the passengers were probably repaid by the excitement of the chase for their being kept two or three hours late in getting to Oban. So that Corryvreckan is still believed in amongst its nearest neighbours.

Mr. Brown came aft abruptly.

"Take this gun," he said.

The Member for Slow, who was contemplatively smoking a very large meerschaum, while his right hand rested on the tiller, and his eyes were leisurely scanning the long sweep of blue water before us, looked up with amazement. Mr. Brown gave the breech-loader to the Glasgow bailie—who handled it nervously, as a bachelor handles a baby—and said, with decision:

"This is a good opportunity, I think, for my entering into that question of the salaries now given to our clerks in the Customs. In such a matter delay only breeds discontent; and the Government, I am sure, will not be sorry to have the subject calmy, fully, and accurately placed before them by a private member."

Mr. Brown went down into his state-room, with quite a look of earnestness on his face. Presently he reappeared with a bundle of papers in his hand; and then, going towards the taffrail, he proceeded to open the parcel and place on the deck a series of documents, partly written, partly printed, and apparently largely consisting of figures. As they lay there, he gazed at them for a moment; but it was clear that his position was not a pleasant one.

He was uncomfortably seated on the deck, with his legs out at right angles, while his head, in the case of the mainsail jibbing, would have been lost for ever to the State. For some minutes he kept altering his position, until at last he said he would go below, so as to have his papers properly spread out before him.

"And yet," he said, pensively, "isn't it a shame to go below in this weather? You know we shall have plenty of wet days in which we shall be unable to do anything but work indoors, eh, Weyland?"

"Of course," said the Conservative member, "when you are on a cruise in Scotland, you are always safe in laying up something for a rainy day."

Mr. Brown packed up his papers, and took them below. When he came on deck again, he was quite cheerful, and even humorous, and proposed that he should take the helm, to which Mr. Weyland consented, on condition that his friend should give the necessary directions in case the wind should come round on the starboard quarter.

"I know what to do in a cutter," said Mr. Brown, timidly.

"Oh," said Weyland, "you know how to slack off the boom guy, haul in the mainsheet till you get the boom amidships, port the helm, jibe the mainsail; then slack off the mainsheet again, you know, hook the guy on the larboard side, haul taut the starboard runner and tackle, and overhaul the larboard one; same with the topping lift, hoist the head sails, and shift the sheets over."

"After that," said Mr. Brown, "I suppose I'd better throw myself over, too, and complete the thing. If you were to treat a yacht like that, there would not be a tooth left in its head. However, you may keep the tiller, Weyland. It is the only work I ever see you at, and when the rainy weather comes, goodness only knows how you will pass the time. I know I shall never come away again without having something to do during those odd moments that you meet in travelling. It's a sort of mainstay, you know—gives you a sense that you are not altogether idling when you have this work to fall back on. And especially when the work is of a character to remedy a great injustice, and give pleasure to a considerable number of your fellow-beings—then, I say, you feel proud that you cannot be taunted with the mere self-seeking indolence of the holiday-maker."

By this time we had run northward by Luing and Easdale, and Loch Feochan, and were standing in towards the Sound of Kerrara. Twilight was now falling over the islands and the sea, and only a faint show of red in the west showed where the sunset had been. When at length we cast anchor in Oban Bay, pale points of stars were beginning to glimmer on the water, and over there at Kerrara the white ridge of the moon was rising behind the black outline of the island, promising us a lovely night.

CHAPTER VII.

OBAN.

OBAN, as you see it in the dawn of a summer's morning, is fair and beautiful to look upon. In the daytime you find that the capital of the western Highlands, which enthusiastic Scotchmen prefer to Biarritz, or Nice, or Naples, or any other place they do not happen to have seen, consists of a mean-looking row of dirty-white houses, stretching round a semicircular bay, the waters of which have, at certain states of the tide, an ancient and fish-like smell. There are no promenades, avenues, or pleasure-grounds; the chief thoroughfare being the street along the quay, which fronts the shops. Towards the west, however, there are a few little villas perched up on the side of the hills that lie behind the town, and down near the shore there is a big hotel. All these things, including the squalor about the quay, and the unspeakably dingy character of most of the houses and cottages, are transfigured by the early sunlight; and more especially if you are well out in the bay, and looking shoreward, Oban, when seen through the golden mist that floods down upon it from over the eastern hills, has something fine and picturesque about its position, and almost rises to its reputation. For there are green hills and grey crags around it which cannot be made commonplace, and you have only to turn from the plain houses and the grocers' shops to find yourself looking out on the perpetual wonder and loveliness of the blue sea, with the rounded mountains of Mull showing a hundred tints of purple and rose-colour, and the gloomy hills of Morven waking up from the mists of the night to catch the first yellow glimmerings of the sun.

We found the Member for Bourton-in-the-Marsh pensively kicking his heels over the gunwale of the Kittiwake. He had been awakened by the throbbing of the paddles of some great steamer, and had gone on deck to have a look at the new district into which he had ventured. He had been up for nearly two hours, had done nothing, and was a little peevish.

"What does Professor Blackie mean," he remarked, with some exaggeration of emphasis, "by writing a song about the gaieties of Oban in the season? Does he know what it is to delude travellers, and entice respectable English people away from their homes by calling a dirty fishing village a watering-place? This a watering-place, is it? I say, Weyland, how will you get the Kittiwake cleaned when you take her out of this hole of a bay?"

After breakfast, however, the amiable nature of his disposition asserted itself; and as he leaned his back against the rattlins, and calmly smoked a cigar, he began to approve of Oban, of the Highlands, of yachting. He even hinted to the Member for Slow that Conservatism had its good points. He told the Glasgow bailie that the Scotch should be proud of their mountains and lochs. He hoped the Queen would soon get better. Then he proposed we should all go ashore, have a look at Oban, and walk across to Dunstaffnage Castle.

Mr. Brown himself steered the pinnace into the quay, and managed it so cleverly as to receive a compliment, which he accepted gravely. Indeed, when we had got on shore to inspect Oban, the practised eye might have detected the least thing of a lurch in Mr. Brown's walk, as of a man who had been accustomed to pace the quarter-deck. His dress, too, was rather nautical in appearance, so that at this moment he might have had his portrait taken as Admiral Brown, M.P. But he never ventured to say anything about shivering his timbers; and as for a hornpipe, Mr. Brown's waist had disappeared about the time that the great Reform Bill was passed.

The few miles of road from Oban to Dunstaffnage led us through the most charming variety of scenery, beginning with a stretch of deep umbrageous wood, and thereafter taking us out into the daylight, and skirting the base of a series of wild and heathery hills. Something less than half way we reached a small fresh-water lake, girt round about by sedges in which Mr. Brown declared there must be moor-hens. Occasionally we met a group of the small and picturesque Highland cattle which are a godsend to the landscape painter; and so thoroughly had those small-headed, rough-coated, and sharp-horned brutes acquired the independent notions of their native land, that our companion the Glasgow bailie regarded with some trepidation their attitude, as they stood in the middle of the road and firmly looked at the strangers. Mr. Brown, however, was brave with the courage of ignorance. He had never been chased down a hill-side by a "stot," or landed in a burn by the horns of a wicked little bull; and so, with the utmost confidence he charged and routed the various phalanxes that opposed our progress, and scarcely walked any the more proudly because of his victory.

In due time we came once more in sight of the

sea, lying dark and blue along the lonely shores of Ossian's Morven. Nearer at hand lay the green island of Lismore, with here and there a nameless lump of dark rock jutting out of the rippling water around it. But when we got further towards the west, so that we saw the magnificent line of jagged mountains stretching all along the northern horizon, the enthusiasm of Mr. Brown could not be expressed in words. There were great white clouds floating rapidly over from the west, so that every moment the colours of the mountains were changing, and while the sunlight fell here and there among the peaks that rise in Morven and Appin, far beyond Loch Etive and up by Glencoe, some mighty mass of rock would grow dark and near, as if cowering under a thunder-cloud. Here and there, too, we could see some of those black clouds break into a grey fleece of rain and quietly erase a mountain from the picture; and then, again, its green sides would come glimmering through the wet, and a faint rainbow would appear to touch the thin line of lake at the mountain's foot.

At length we got down to the sea, and to the rocky headland on which stand the massive ruins of Dunstaffnage.

"To tell you the truth," said Mr. Brown, "I do not care for ruins—I do not care for anything—when I can turn to this wonderful picture of the sea and mountains and lochs. The more I look at it, the more I am inclined to register an awful vow never to return to a town again. Why should a man devote himself to the public good until he is just ready to drop into his coffin? I have done my share. I have a great mind never to return to London, but to have a small house built on this very promontory, and live here within the sound of the sea—until—until the time comes when I shall hear no more sounds. Besides what use am I—except to make one of a majority that is already so big as to make the Ministry a deal too cheeky? If we had a struggling Government, do you think we should have had all that hocus pocus about Epping Forest? Well, after all, you want independent members to look after those things. Perhaps I should better fulfil my duty by going back into the old track. I venture to hope that some of my countrymen owe something to my efforts in Parliament; and I know that in this matter of the Customs Clerks' grievances, I am working towards a most praiseworthy end. Forgive my talking about myself, Weyland, but I have often remarked that the sight of mountains and the sea—of the great powers of nature—forces on a man questions about his own position, and causes him to review his relations with the world. Thank you; the last was as good a cigar as a man ever smoked."

My friend was rather reserved and thoughtful during the walk to Oban, but he brightened up after dinner, and proposed we should go on shore to play a game of billiards at the hotel. As the pinnace slowly cleft its way through the dark water, the blades of the oar shedding gleams of phosphoric fire on each side, Mr. Brown remarked that both moon and stars were invisible.

Indeed, before we reached the shore, a few drops of rain were falling.

"Is not that most fortunate?" said he. "Just as I was beginning to accuse myself of idleness, there comes the wet day which will enable me to get some work done. To-morrow—yes, to-morrow—I will redeem the promises I have made to myself—and so, Weyland, let us have a merry evening; and you will give me 30 in 100, and I will play you for a sovereign."

CHAPTER VIII.

FROM OBAN TO JURA.

WHERE was the rain? Were we really in the Highlands? When breakfast called us into the saloon the sun was shining down through the painted colours of the skylight, and throwing streaks of crimson and blue on the decorated sides of the cabin. Mr. Brown, M.P., professed himself profoundly disgusted. He regarded the sunlight as if it were his mortal enemy.

"Another day handed over to idleness," he remarked, with a beautiful affectation of anger; "for, you know, Weyland, a man cannot be expected to stop downstairs in this hot weather, and study a batch of figures. You can't do it. I am sure that matter of the salaries of those unfortunate Customs Clerks wants serious inquiry; but how can you go into it on a broiling day, and in the limited space which even your handsome saloon affords?"

Indeed, when we got up on deck, the rain, for which Mr. Brown declared himself so anxious, seemed further off than ever. The Kittiwake was already speeding away southward from Oban, her tall white sails filled with a brisk westerly breeze, and overhead there was a dark blue sky that had its light reflected in the ruffled plain that lay all around us. Out before us—for we went round Kerrara before going south—the lofty mountains of Mull were gradually becoming more distinct, until we could see the glimmering of streams in the deep gullies, and here and there a small white cottage along the lonely shores. In our wake stretched the far-reaching arms of Loch Etive and Loch Linnhe—long blue creeks lying underneath the wild mountains of Morven and Appin, and embracing the lower and greener hills of Lismore. It was a fair and beautiful picture—the brisk blue ripple of the water, the innumerable islands, the flocks of sea-birds floating on the waves or dashing this way and that against the westerly winds, while up in the north stood the calm and silent rampart of the mountains, touched here and there with the shadow of a cloud.

"There is no sign of rain," remarked my friend, scanning the horizon with a wistful glance. "That haze you see along the mountains is never accompanied by rain, and yet there was rain last night."

He turned with a well-simulated sigh to light a cigar, and then he caught sight of a bundle of newspapers that had been brought on board that morning. Lazily he opened them; but suddenly he announced to us, in a voice of astonishment, that the Lords had thrown out the Ballot Bill. Weyland, sitting by the tiller, looked up. I became apprehensive of a skirmish between the Member for Slow and the Member for Bourton-in-the-Marsh.

"Poor old things," said Mr. Brown, with an accent of contemptuous tenderness. "I don't wonder at their being in a hurry for their holidays; and nobody ought to grudge them the sense of importance with which they will now go down into the country. It will be something to keep up the spirits of the amiable old gentlemen as they drive about the country roads in closed-up old-fashioned yellow chariots, and answer with a paralytic nod the salutations of the farmers. I hope the old gentlemen will keep up their system and get strong. They will want some strength of digestion next Session for the operation known as eating the leek."

The wrath on Weyland's face was terrible to look upon, and he was fairly speechless with rage. The Glasgow bailie turned from the one to the other with uneasy glances, probably fearing that Weyland might in the recklessness of passion shoot the Kittiwake high and dry on the nearest island.

"Perhaps," said the Member for Slow, with a wild and ghastly effort to accomplish a smile, " you will introduce a Bill for the removal of the House of Lords to Hanwell. Or perhaps you'd have them sent to a pauper school to teach them to write their own names."

"Most of 'em can't," said Mr. Brown coolly. He was trying to make out whether a certain big bird, down near Ardincaple Point, was a gull or a solan.

"I am not surprised at anything that is done by the Liberal party," said Mr. Weyland hotly, "when I hear the perfectly reckless and inconsiderate way in which individual members talk of the most vital institutions of the country—as if they were mere foot-balls to be kicked about for the convenience of a Premier or the amusement of a session. I do not know whether it is thoughtlessness or ignorance——"

"It's a solan!" exclaimed Mr. Brown.

The bird had gone down with a sudden rush, and we could see the water leap thirty feet into the air with the fierce plunge. Then the snow-white, long-winged solan rose once more, made one or two slow circles, and finally came sailing up towards the north. Mr. Brown darted down to the cabin; and presently reappeared with a double-barrelled breech-loader in his hand.

"If I could only get one of those magnificent birds," said he, "I'd give up the notion of making a collection. When you have got the King, you do not care about the Court."

And, in truth, this particular solan, forgetting the shyness of its tribe, seemed determined to give Mr. Brown a chance. It flew at a great height, but it came slowly up in a direct line across the boat. Mr. Brown's eyes were fixed with a painful anxiety on the slow pinions of the gannet as it came nearer and nearer; and he was heard to whisper an agitated question as to whether a swan-shot cartridge would reach that height. None of us dared answer him; even Weyland had forgotten the cruelties heaped on the House of Lords in the excitement caused by the approach of the solan. Mr. Brown stealthily put up the gun to his shoulder —just as if he were some fat old sportsman in the Black Forest nervously expecting the appearance of a roebuck. So dazzling was the clear blue that it was difficult to follow the slow flight of the large bird; and it seemed to be overhead while yet Mr. Brown would not fire. Mr. Weyland began to be agitated about the safety of the rigging, and would probably have interposed but that the startling bang of Mr. Brown's right barrel told us that the great event was decided one way or the other.

"I have shot him—I have killed him—I have smashed him up!" shouted the Member for Bourton-in-the-Marsh, with the most unstatesmanlike and unsportsmanlike eagerness. Certainly the bird had disappeared to leeward. Mr. Brown sprang behind the mainsail, and lo! some hundred yards ahead, an immense white thing floated on the water. He shouted that the bird was dead. He implored Weyland to get a small boat ready. He gave various orders, couched in the language of Cockaigne, to the astonished sailors, who had been regarding the falling solan with little interest. And then, in the middle of all this turmoil, a loud laugh was heard from Weyland, and the solan was seen to flutter up from the water and continue its flight.

Despair fell over the countenance of my amiable friend. He did not utter a word; but he was calmly relinquishing himself to his fate, when the solan was seen to "tower" for a few yards. Mr. Brown apparently imagined that this natural phenomenon was but the beginning of a long excursion on the part of the solan, and was, indeed, turning away in disgust, when the bird fell straight into the water, and floated on the waves a lifeless and dishevelled mass of feathers. Some few minutes afterwards, Mr. Brown was regarding with inexpressible delight and wonder the monster of the deep which lay before him, with its snow-white wings extended on the deck. He called our attention to the beautiful colours on its long and powerful beak, to the shading on its legs, to the immense breadth of its wings. One of the men further gratified Mr. Brown by informing him that the wings of the solan were sometimes found to be seven feet across, and that no other bird so much resembled an albatross. The hero of the hour regarded his prize with a new interest—there were wild and poetical associations about this magnificent creature that he had brought down. It was with some hesitation that he allowed it to be taken below, Weyland giving orders that it should be packed and forwarded to Glasgow by the first steamer they could intercept. Mr. Brown hoped they were able to stuff large birds in Glasgow.

The slaughter of the solan was a fortunate thing for us all. Mr. Brown's geniality, in consequence of his exploit, was excessive; nothing could exceed his politeness, his good-nature, and his efforts to amuse us. He doubtless felt that we ought all to share in his joy, and he even went the length of tendering a formal apology to Mr. Weyland for his remarks about the House of Lords, which the Member for Slow accepted with one of his prodigious laughs. And so, in this delightful state of affairs, the long summer day passed pleasantly, and we gradually drew down towards Jura, keeping well outside the islands of Gavelock and Scarba. Here we experienced a rather heavy sea; but the Kittiwake conducted herself with propriety, and Mr. Brown, though he was occasionally silent and solemn, never had to go below.

Out to windward lay the desolate-looking islands of Colonsay and Oronsay, amid the ceaseless wash of the Atlantic. Why that lengthy ballad of Dr. Leyden should have taken such hold of my friend from the South, it was impossible to say; but he continued to gaze on the bleak and distant shores of Colonsay all the time we were creeping along the coast of Jura. And when at last we anchored in Loch Tarbet, and found almost over our heads the immense and gloomy peaks that are known to fishermen as the Paps of Jura, we could see that the "Song of Colonsay" was still sounding its melancholy refrain in the ears of Mr. Brown. But whenever he grew too sad, the least mention of the solan woke him up into life again; and all that evening, as we sate on deck, and smoked, and watched the stars glimmering on the sea around us that was black as night with the shadows of the mountains, his talk was of the wonders of the deep that are known to sailors, and of the rough sports and enjoyments that might be got at if one were only young enough to become a middy.

CHAPTER IX.

DEER-STALKING IN JURA.

A COLD grey mist was rising off the bay, and masses of watery-looking clouds were slowly creeping up the dark sides of the mountains, when Mr. Brown, M.P., stepped on deck and took his accustomed glance round, apparently to see if there was a chance of rain. The prospect was gloomy. The waters of the sound were rough and grey; Islay was half hidden in mist; and overhead there was a dense pall of vapour through which the sun could not pierce. Despite the fact that the Member for Bourton-in-the-Marsh had been longing for rain, in order that he might devote himself to the question of the Customs Clerks' grievances, he did not seem pleased to find it so near. He looked at the clean deck and spars of the Kittiwake, and complained that a yacht looked clammy on a cold morning. With a morose sort of poetry he compared her to a sea-bird floating on the water in time of rain, with her wings folded closely up, and her appearance dejected. He remarked that there was much gloomy grandeur about the Jura mountains; but that, once you had seen them, there was no use in remaining under their cold and oppressive shadows. He observed that the Sound of Jura was a melancholy piece of water; and was of opinion that the Hebrides generally seemed a sterile region, visited by fogs and rains and the cold wash of the sea.

But a great surprise was in store for my friend. While we were regarding the desolate prospect around us, the pinnace of the Kittiwake was observed to be coming out from the shore; and in the stem sat Mr. Weyland, himself. There was a bluff satisfaction in his face. He sprang up the gangway quite lightly, and slapped Mr. Brown on the back.

"You've heard me speak of Maclean of Hulishtaveg?" he said.

"No, I have not," replied Mr. Brown, coldly; for he did not like to be slapped on the back.

"No matter, he sends you his compliments in very good English, and offers you as much red deer shooting as you like, and says you will get men, dogs, and guns up at Glen-cona an hour hence."

"Red deer!" exclaimed Mr. Brown, with an awe-struck look.

And with that he darted down the companion to see if breakfast was laid. He implored us to make haste. He scalded his mouth with coffee. He said it would have been hard if we had gone away from the Hebrides without slaying a red deer, and talked with such animation and excitement about that noble sport, and about the grandeur of this lonely island of Jura, and of the more than royal hospitality exercised by the brave and courteous Highland gentlemen who live in those wilds, that we half expected to see tears of admiration start into his eyes. Weyland, improved the time by detailing the qualifications of the deer-stalker—how that he must have the eye of a hawk, the pertinacity of a sleuth-hound, the footing of a chamois —how that he must be brave and patient, nimble and agile, and prepared to suffer any privation. We observed that as Mr. Brown rose to go up on deck before us, he buttoned his coat tightly round what was once a waist, erected his head, and assumed a look of bright and sharp activity. His efforts to improve his figure, however, were a failure.

It took us nearly an hour to reach the plain white house which had been pointed out to us as Glen-cona—a solitary building, perched up on an open space of morass which led the way into a deep gap between the hills. Not only were the gillies and dogs in readiness, but the Maclean himself—a tall and spare-built man, with long white hair and flowing beard—had come up from his house to receive his friend's friends. This he did with a simple and yet stately courtesy which greatly impressed Mr. Brown, who subsequently informed us that he could not help thinking the old man with the white beard, and the lofty manners and the peculiar inflection of English, was a descendant of Ossian. Hulishtaveg was not in kilts, but his gillies were—the big, weather-tanned men who stood silently by, except when they rebuked one of the shaggy and splendid-looking deerhounds, and who received from their master a glass of whisky, which was no great length of time in reaching its destination. When the Maclean had given the men certain instructions in what was apparently graphic and forcible Gaelic, he bade us farewell in a few words of very fair English, and took his departure.

Weyland now impressed on the head keeper that everything was to be done to give Mr. Brown a shot—that he was to be considered the chief of the party. When the swarthy and bearded gillie was at length made to understand this, he simply laid hold of Mr. Brown and treated him as if he were a child, with a quiet, good-natured patronage that my friend knew not how to resent. In the first place, he insisted on the Member for Bourton-in-the

Marsh leaving behind him a white coat which he wore, and putting on instead a brown jacket which one of the gillies was ordered to strip off his shoulders. Mr. Brown objected, but his protestations were of no avail.

"Cash pless me!" said the keeper, "it will pe for no use if you go up sa hill wi' a big, white, starin' coat on, that will pe seen through the length and sa preadth o' Jura. Wass you neffer after sa deer afore?"

Mr. Brown had to confess that he had never before hunted the wild deer or followed the roe; whereupon the big keeper helped my friend into the gillie's jacket, and slung a telescope over his shoulder, and bound a cartridge-belt round his waist; but the rifle which was apportioned to him was handed over to one of the men. Then we set out. Mr. Brown grinned a ghastly grin over his costume and accoutrements; but he was evidently feeling a little nervous.

For the first part of our journey our way lay along a marshy hollow that formed the base of two hills; and every few minutes as we advanced, the man in front, who had a brace of deerhounds in slips, would startle a big black-cock or put up a pack of grouse, the sudden sound of which made Mr. Brown jump. It was the only noise that broke the profound stillness of this solitary glen; we could not even hear a stream trickling down the mountain-side. Then we began to ascend the hill—in some places so steep that our hands were about as serviceable as our feet. What with hopping over bits of bog, and climbing over rocks, and working through bracken, Mr. Brown was looking rather exhausted as we neared the summit; but here a halt was called, and the plan of operations formed.

The Member for Bourton-in-the-Marsh now became the hero of the hour, and, with a face that seemed to us a little pale, he crept up to a line of rock on the top of the hill, and there lay down, his rifle by his side. He unslung his telescope. He gently put the end of it over the rock, and for several anxious minutes was seen to regard the valley opposite him. Then he came back shaking his head.

The keeper stole up to the same place, without any telescope, and after a keen look, beckoned on Mr. Brown to follow him. What was the meaning of that abrupt movement? Mr. Brown dropped his telescope, and took up his rifle; the keeper seized the latter, took it off the rock, and turned to his companion with a look of anger and surprise.

"Cash pless me!" we heard him exclaim in an excited whisper, "Wass you going to fire? Sa stag iss a mile away, and a' sa hinds are watchin' up by sa burn. You will have to go down sa hill again, and along sa glen, and up by sa burn, and through sa trees—it will be three miles you will go afore you wass to get near him."

But nothing would daunt Mr. Brown, now that he had seen his quarry. In mingled trepidation and excitement he came back and told us upon what an awful venture he was setting out. We agreed to watch his progress from the ambush on the top of the hill; while he and the gillie with the dogs went off on their circuit so as to get at the stag. He left us his telescope, and took with him our blessing.

More than an hour elapsed before we caught sight of them, and then we made out two tiny figures stealing along the opposite side of the valley. A stretch of fir-wood lay between them and the stag; and it was evident that the success of the expedition depended on Mr. Brown being able to get through this wood without attracting the attention of his prey. A grave and watchful gillie who followed every movement with intensest interest expressed his opinion that the "shentleman tit not know much of sa shooting and would pe sure to make a noise in sa fir." At length we saw Mr. Brown, creeping on hands and knees, glide into the plantation of young firs and disappear. The stag still stood about thirty yards from the other side of the wood, in a little gully where there was probably some water, while two or three hinds were on a grassy plateau above him, walking about and occasionally nibbling the herbage. Our excitement was now so great that no one spoke. A dead silence prevailed. Suddenly there was a light pattering heard near us, and the next moment a hind came cantering down in front of us. The moment she saw us a sort of paralysis seemed to overtake her. She halted for one second, all her limbs quivering; then she was off with the speed of lightning, followed by two hinds and two stags that had been quietly coming on in Indian file. All this had occurred in an instant; and in the same instant Weyland had started up, cocked his rifle, and fired. The gillie fired. The second stag, at which the gillie had shot, gave one spring into the air and tumbled forward lifeless; but the first stag, Weyland's quarry, after having gone down on its fore-knees, struggled up again, and was seen to make straight down the hill. "Oh, sa tawgs, sa tawgs, what for had we no sa tawgs wi us, tamernation and diabhol!" shouted the gillie, and then he dashed down the hill-side after the wounded deer, Weyland, himself long-legged and active, vainly endeavouring to keep up with his extraordinary speed. When they had disappeared, I turned to the other valley, where also the crack of a rifle had been heard. What was that distant and corpulent little figure doing, but waving a handkerchief and dancing a wild fandango of delight, while the gillie was choking off the hounds that were apparently bent on attacking some brown object lying there? Apparently the man had divined that the dogs might be wanted elsewhere, for presently we saw him disappear with them round the head of the glen, while Mr. Brown, still waving a handkerchief, descended to the burn, crossed over, and slowly began to ascend the hill. Long before he had reached the top he had shouted the joyous news, and when he arrived, speechless, smothered in perspiration, covered with brown moss-water, and dishevelled beyond expression, he reserved his last energies for a wild performance of a Highland reel, and then sank, glorious and happy, on the heather.

"Killed him—killed him—killed him!" he cried, "dead as a stone—big as a house—want two ponies to fetch him home—I'll have him stuffed if I pay a thousand ounds for it!"

"With a gold medal slung round his neck—*Shot by Pisistratus Brown, Esq., M.P., in the mountains of Jura, August,* 1871."

Mr. Brown lay on the heather, took deep draughts of the clear and cool air, and rubbed his hands. Already he pictured to himself the noble animal standing in the hall of a certain house in Holland-park the admiration and wonder of all visitors. He was too much excited, indeed, to give any account of how he had shot the deer, and that did not leak out until Weyland, the head keeper, and the gillie with the dogs had all returned to us. They, too, were in an exultant mood. The hounds had hunted down the wounded stag until they had brought him to bay, and he was found facing them, when Weyland got up in time to give him another bullet. The gillie had brought down a very tolerable stag, but Weyland's prey turned out to be a hart of magnificent proportions, with horns that the keeper described in technical language which considerably puzzled the Member for Bourton-in-the-Marsh. When we came to ask what sort of horns he had secured, there came the ominous confession that the animal he had shot was not adorned in that way.

"It wass a hind," said the gillie, with some contempt. "Sa stag will pe neffer touched at all."

"But you can't deny it's a deer," said Mr. Brown, almost fiercely, "and if I didn't get the stag, whose fault was it, Donald, or Duncan, or MacTavish or whatever is your name? Answer me that! The plain story, Weyland, is simply this—that your confounded shooting startled the stag just as I was getting out of the wood. The beggar was off before you could have winked —like a flash of powder—and I saw him join the whole herd of 'em, and off they went. What could I do? By Jove, I banged into the whole of 'em, just as any man would, and you should have seen the cracker that deer went when I caught him——"

"Her," said Weyland, cruelly.

"Her or him, what's the difference? You may talk of spires and harts, and stags and calves; but all I know is I've shot a deer, and as that sort of thing doesn't fall in my way every day, I may confess that I'm uncommonly proud of it, and, with the permission of Allasterbeg, or whatever you call him, I propose to give these Macdonalds, and Macdougals, and MacTavishes here a sovereign apiece."

Mr. Brown now became anxious that the two ponies which had been sent for should arrive, that we might go down the glen in triumph; but as the day had worn on with our repeated delays, it was resolved to go down quietly to Mr. Maclean's house, and carry him on board the Kittiwake. Hulishtaveg was well pleased with the story of the day's performances, and remarked on the good fortune which had attended what was, after all, an experiment.

"Sa morn's morning," he said to Mr. Brown, "you will pe early afoot, and teil sa fears but you will come home wis a fine good stag—as good as any one in Jura."

"I will get up at three o'clock," said Mr. Brown, eagerly; "and you know, Mr. Maclean, I am a stranger to this sort of thing, and if, after dinner, you could give me a hint or two, you know ——"

Hulishtaveg gave us after dinner something much better—a Gaelic song about a young person called Maggie, who was asked to marry a certain red-haired William; and this he sung in a shrill, quavering voice that had some faint resemblance to the reediness of the bagpipes.

CHAPTER X.

DEER-DRIVING IN JURA.

THE cold light of the dawn was beginning to steal down into the glens, and there was a faint saffron colour becoming visible in the sky, far over the tops of the mountains, when Mr. Brown, M.P., stood on the deck of the Kittiwake and saw the pinnace being brought round. Much of the enthusiasm of the previous evening had gone. The visions begotten of Hulishtaveg's stories of deer-stalking, salmon-spearing, and otter-hunting were now cold, and grey, and faint in the clear light of the early morning; and Mr. Brown was no longer ready to scoff at late sleepers, and to expatiate on the delight of getting out of bed while the mists were still in the valleys and the darkness not yet lifted off the far and murmuring plain of the sea.

He was very silent, and even gloomy; and, as he sat in the stern of the pinnace, looked wistfully over to the distant shores of Islay, where man and nature seemed still buried in sleep.

The Member for Slow, more accustomed to sportsman's hours, was, on the contrary, full of facetious humours, and strove to impress on Mr. Brown the awful nature of the excitement experienced by the man who finds deer running by in front of him, while he endeavours to single out the finest hart for his shot. He impressed on his friend, too, the gratitude he owed to Maclean of Hulishtaveg for getting up this drive in his honour—a form of deer-shooting rarely resorted to on account of the number of men required, and the tendency it has to make the deer wild and frighten them into neighbouring territory.

"I dare say the old man started at 2 o'clock this morning to arrange the drive," remarked Mr. Weyland. "And how would you like going up those wild glens in the middle of the night, with mist-clouds making the most familiar places dangerous to you?"

"I don't see the necessity," said the Member for Bourton-in-the-Marsh, morosely. "You don't expect to catch the deer asleep, do you? And when you turn a man out at four o'clock and thrust him into the raw air of the morning, and make him swallow his breakfast before he has got any appetite, you upset him for the day, that's all. You may call it sport; I call it a mistake. I can get up as early as most men—when there's any need; but to be lugged out in the middle of the night merely because it's considered fine, and sportsmanlike, and heroic, is a very different thing. I would very much rather have spent the next two hours in studying those grievances of the Customs clerks, and getting some useful work done. However, as that old idiot of a Highlandman, I dare say, has been rampaging about the whole country-side since midnight, I suppose we needn't waste any time in getting up to the starting-point."

It was most ungenerous of Mr. Brown to speak thus of his benefactor, who had not only arranged for him a day's sport such as few men, be they

Princes or Cabinet Ministers, are privileged to enjoy, but had also sent down a horse and two ponies for us. The Glasgow bailie was to have accompanied us; but on rousing him about 3.30 he had uttered the most solemn vows that he would see us anywhere before he would budge an inch, so that we had to leave him to his inglorious rest. Accordingly the horse and the ponies carried us picturesquely, if not comfortably, up to Glencona, where we found Hulishtaveg, one or two gillies, and the dogs. The rest of the gillies and hillmen had started an hour before for a district lying considerably beyond that in which we had been successful the day before. No time was to be lost. We got into the saddle again—Mr. Maclean stoutly resisting Weyland's invitation to change places with him—and set off up the marshy glen that led into the mountains.

In reply to Mr. Brown, Hulishtaveg informed us that we should have a terribly hot day; but in the meantime the morning was clear and rather chilly. There was a rawness in the air around us, although far overhead we could see the sunlight strike the eastward-looking sides of the mountains. But the jolting of the white pony which he bestrode had brought some warmth into Mr. Brown's frame; and a tolerably lengthy pull at a whisky-flask, which had gone the round of the circle at Glencona, had brought more liveliness into his eye and talk. He began to feel more sure about being able to distinguish between a hind and hart as the deer went by. He was quite certain he would not fire prematurely, and kill some harmless little animal running in front of its mother. He would take the greatest care not to frighten the hinds, so that they might turn and drive back the stags. Not for the world would he spoil sport.

"And, mirover," said old Hulishtaveg, in his shrill and curious English, "it may pe sa stags will come first. When sey get a great fright, sometimes sa stag will come afore sa hinds, espaycially if he sinks some danger is apout; and all you will do, Mester Prown, iss no to put yoursel' into a hurry, but tek your time—tek your time—and fire weel forrit."

"I'll fire a yard ahead of 'em," said Mr. Brown confidently. "Only give me a chance, and you'll see."

"A chance?" said the old Highlandman rather testily, "no man will pe able to make a chance for you if sa deer will not be inclined to go your way; but sa men knaw as much apoot sa deer as ony men in sa country; and if you do not get a fine, big, braw pair o' horns, it will pe your own fault, sir, neversaless and mirover."

When, at length, we had got within about a mile of our points of ambush we dismounted, and the horse and ponies were left in charge of a small boy in kilts. Then the gillies—all but he with the dogs—went off to join in that gentle pressing of the deer in a particular direction, which is a much more difficult business than merely shooting at them when they come to you. The manner in which a few men—keeping themselves, as a rule, invisible—will succeed in driving a herd of deer in a certain line, is most marvellous, and is all the more so that the exploit is so seldom performed. The Maclean himself undertook to post the three strangers; and when this was done, and we had all received ample instructions and injunctions, the old man departed, rifle in hand, to seek out a corner for himself. His whispered directions were the last sound we heard; then followed the strange and dead stillness that reigned over the broad valley, and we were left to peer anxiously from our hiding-places and await the coming of the deer.

I could see Mr. Brown. He was placed behind a rock in a little ravine, which had once been the bed of a stream. He had placed his cap by his side, so that he might peep over the boulders before him, and the shining bald head gleamed like a piece of smooth quartz down among the grey shadows of the schist. He was furnished with a double-barrel breech-loading rifle that Weyland had had made for him in Edinburgh; and he had received the most impressive instructions not to fire within a mile of my station should the deer escape him and come up that way. Weyland, with a gillie and the deer-hounds, was posted, so far as we could make out Hulishtaveg's explanation, on the other side of the hill, in the direction the deer were likely to take if fired at by us.

How long we waited it is impossible to say. It seemed ages, and it was probably hours. At last there appeared by the side of a clump of trees high up on the opposite hill the flutter of a white handkerchief which was instantly withdrawn—the signal that the deer were in sight. Mr. Brown put the barrels of his gun carefully on the ledge of rock before him.

And then, in the death-like silence, we saw the first of the deer appear. They were two full-grown hinds and a calf, that came lightly and gently cantering over the moss and heather, stopping now and again to look back, with their ears erect, and their long lithe throats arching up their small heads. Presently came three more hinds, in single file, and then two stags, a small one and a large one, the latter with splendid horns. It was an exciting moment; for it was impossible to say which way they might go. They had evidently been alarmed by the gillies somewhere; but to so slight a degree that they trotted gently, and stopped every two or three seconds to look back, which they did with their nostrils high in the air, and their ears thrown forward. A more picturesque group was never painted by Landseer; but what we chiefly thought of, doubtless, was their distance from us.

As we watched them, in this anxious fashion, one of the hinds trotted off to the right, and the others at some distance followed her, one by one. They were now apparently going straight over the opposite hill, and how was one gillie to intercept them? Suddenly we saw him start from his hiding-place, throw his jacket into the air, and halloo at the pitch of his voice. The whole herd now sprung down the hill, and headed down the glen. Here another gillie started from some unknown ambush; and the stags, now in front, turned once more, and made straight for our ambush. Now or never was our chance. On they came with those light elastic strides that seemed to skip the ground, the smaller stag now leading. How different was this terrible pace from the slow rumbling of the pasteboard stag at Wimbledon, which Mr. Brown had been declaring the night before he could hit in the heart five times out of six! But if the pace was trying, the line they took was advantageous; and in far less time than it has taken to write these words they were upon us. Bang! went Mr. Brown's first barrel. The smaller stag cleared the rocky channel at one leap, and was making down into the hollow of the glen, when a shot—from a quarter which modesty directs shall be nameless—sent him head first into a patch of long green grass that surrounded a mountain spring. Almost simultaneously with that shot, Mr. Brown fired his second barrel, and lo! the larger stag did actually stumble forward and then fall heavily on his side. Mr. Brown uttered a startling yell, and dashed down the rocky chasm, over boulders and stones and trunks of trees. The stag rose on its fore feet, and again it fell. In vain I shouted to my frantic friend not to go near the deer; for the next moment I saw him aim a blow at the head of his adversary with the butt end of Weyland's valuable rifle. Again and again the excited sportsman flourished his weapon, and then he sat down on the slain deer's neck, and took hold of its antlers, and waved the butt of the rifle over his head.

"Why," said he, when I got up, "did you ever see the like of that? Two stags—one with each barrel!"

I calmly regarded my friend. He blushed a little, and then said, uneasily,

"Do you think you shot the first one?"

"Do you think you shot it?" I asked.

He looked away for a second or two; and then he said, reflectively,

"Perhaps, after all, I may have been mistaken. At all events I can afford to give you that one,

I have enough. I wouldn't quarrel with any one about a wretched deer. The man who spoils a day's sport by claiming what isn't his own—bah! I have no patience with him. Well, what is the matter?"

The last words were uttered rather angrily. The fact was that Mr. Brown had put out one of his legs over the fallen deer, but not so artistically as to conceal the fact that the stag had been shot in his hind legs—the ball going through both, and smashing them.

"If you consider," said he, "the pace he was going at, the wonder is that any mortal man could have got near him. I'm not proud. I hit a deer where I can; and I'm satisfied if I kill him. I suppose it isn't every man who can say that out of three shots he killed two deer, eh?"

Indeed, Mr. Brown, M.P., forgot this flaw in his happiness, amid the universal congratulations of his companions. He would not, he said, trouble Mr. Maclean's gillies to go any further that day. He was satisfied. Sport, not indiscriminate slaughter, was his object. And there and then he invited all the gillies to a supper at Glencona, and forthwith begged Weyland to lend him a dozen of champagne. Of that supper, which came off about eight o'clock, it is impossible to speak here. Certainly no more strange, and motley, and picturesque gathering was ever before summoned to drink dry sillery amid the dusky solitudes of Jura.

CHAPTER XI.

GROUSE-SHOOTING IN JURA.

It is not every day that a Highland laird has the opportunity of entertaining two members of our Imperial Legislature; and whether it was that circumstance, or merely the amiable temperament of Mr. Brown, M.P., that affected Hulishtaveg, certain it is that the chieftain was excessively courteous to us. Not content with allowing the strangers from the Kittiwake to slay his deer, he now proposed that the Member for Bourton-in-the Marsh should undertake a day's grouse shooting. Mr. Brown regarded this invitation with a complacent serenity. It was a compliment to his powers as a sportsman. It is true he spoke in rather a contemptuous tone about grouse. The man who was able to bring down a stag at full speed might be pardoned for considering the whole grouse family, even including the capercailzie, as rather small game. But Mr. Brown was not proud. He thanked the Maclean with a gracious politeness, and said he would go on the next morning, if it did not rain.

"A trap o' rain will not do much harm," said the old highlander, unnecessarily taking a look round the horizon, on which all the evidences of settled weather were apparent. "You wass very fortunate, mirover, wis your two days at sa deer. You will not expect to have aye such goot weather among sa Jura hills."

"But you don't understand, Mr. Maclean," said my friend, gravely. "A member of parliament, whether he be in the Cabinet or a mere outsider, never wholly gets rid of his duties by leaving town. A portion of his leisure, at least, he owes to his countrymen. And I am now investigating a most important question, with a view to remedying a great grievance—that, namely, of the capricious and unsatisfactory manner in which salaries are awarded to her Majesty's clerks of Customs in the East of London and elsewhere. Should a change in the weather occur I must devote myself to this matter, grouse or no grouse, red deer or no red deer."

"Oh, ferry well, ferry well," said old Hulishtaveg, "no goot will come to sa man who neglects his pusiness for his amusements, mirover."

On this occasion there was no picturesque procession of ponies and gillies, for our beat began about half a mile from the bay in which the Kittiwake was moored. Most of this half mile lay round the shore; and Mr. Brown—as he listened vaguely to Weyland's comparison of the virtues of pointers and setters—let his eye rove over the blue expanse of sea that lay smooth and still around the coasts of Islay. The Sound, that is generally swept by currents of wind coming down the gorge between the Jura mountains and the Islay shore, was almost glass-like. There was scarcely a breath of wind, and it was apparent that we should have warm work of it on the moors.

"Why here is Mr. Maclean again," said Mr. Brown, as we neared the trysting-place. "The old man seems to think we could not start without his coming to see us off, and give us a glass of whisky. I wonder if he thinks a member of Parliament an extraordinary creature."

I ventured to hint to Mr. Brown that Hulishtaveg's courtesy took its rise in the immemorial traditions of his class, and was not dictated by a profound reverence for the British Parliament. Doubtless, however, the old man was not displeased to see his name in the Edinburgh and Glasgow papers as the host of the representatives of two important English boroughs.

Hulishtaveg wished us good luck, and then we set off for the base of the nearest hill, accompanied by two gillies, a boy, two brace of setters, a pointer and a retriever. The head keeper explained to us that this pointer, which had been presented to Hulishtaveg by an English gentleman, was a steady old dog that was likely to be of excellent service to the central gun, when the setters were ranging rather widely. Mr. Brown remarked that he did not care with what sort of dog he shot. He was also indifferent as to whether he were placed on the right, or on the left, or in the middle. He put a couple of cartridges into the barrels of his breech-loader, flung the gun up on his shoulder with quite a jaunty air, and stalked forward erect and confident.

Indeed, Mr. Brown lost none of this ease of manner when a brace of the setters were uncoupled and we began to move cautiously along a piece of swampy ground lying at the base of a smooth green hill.

"Those setters have been badly trained," he remarked, with a cool air. "They are wild. They will put up the birds out of shot. I can foresee that they will. When once we reach the dryer ground, where the grouse are sure to be———"

He never finished the sentence. Old Dan the pointer, who had given himself but one or two brief preliminary scampers, was suddenly seen to curb his pace; and then, after carefully advancing a few yards, he became motionless. As we quickly and stealthily went up to him, he moved not a muscle of his rigid frame—his neck and head stretched forward, his tail stiff as a rod behind, his fore leg hanging motionless in the air. As we got near him, he began to draw on the birds; and, knowing that grouse run swiftly when caught in grassy cover, we were looking well forward, when a magnificent whirr almost underneath Dan's nose was followed by a hurried bang from Mr. Brown's gun. A heap of feathers tumbled on to the ground; and my excitable friend—forgetting the example he was showing to the dogs—rushed madly towards the spot, caught the bird, and flourished it in the air.

But there was one man more excited than Mr. Brown, and that was the gillie. In his first alarm and rage at seeing my companion put up his gun to shoot a black-cock, he had yelled out in Gaelic, and now, in the same language, he was expostulating with Mr. Brown on the appalling nature of his conduct, while Weyland had positively to sit down on a tuft of heather to give vent to prodigious roars of laughter. Mr. Brown looked deeply hurt.

"What have I done?" he said.

In the mildest manner Weyland pointed out that he had fired at a bird which, had it been a grouse, would have belonged to me; that he had killed a black-cock after being warned that the time for shooting that animal had not arrived; and that he had acted in a manner sufficient to have demoralised the best setters or pointers ever bred and trained.

"But, at all events, I have killed the bird," said Mr. Brown gloomily.

He moved forward with less gaiety of demeanour now. The setters which, in spite of his example, had dropped very prettily when the bird rose, now recommenced their light and active labours, and the grave and more cautious Dan, keeping nearer at home, worked the ground between them in a most satisfactory manner. We were now getting up the hill towards a level plateau, and were near the brow of the ascent when we flushed our first pack. They rose to Mr. Brown's side, perhaps at a distance of about twenty yards, and after a start caused by the sudden noise, and a stumbling about the stock of the gun, as if it had caught in his waistcoat, we were surprised to see the long steel barrels pointing in the direction of the now disappearing grouse, and Mr. Brown pulling at the trigger, without a vestige of sound following. Then, with a fearful exclamation of anger, my companion took down the breech-loader and looked at it. He had forgotten to put in a cartridge in place of the one fired at the black cock —indeed, the hammer was still down on the barrel. Weyland did not laugh this time; he was too much annoyed. Mr. Brown's moroseness deepened, and we went on.

One or two members of the pack had loitered behind in the heather on the brow of the hill. Of these a brace fell to Weyland's gun, and one bird, getting up out of shot, made after its companions.

These we resolved on following, but taking care to miss nothing on the way.

It appeared that the pack had been well scattered, for we had just rounded one shoulder of the hill, when up got a fine bird from under a big mass of rock that jutted out from the hill-side. This, also, was Mr. Brown's bird, but two barrels sent after him scarcely caused him to swerve from his course, and we could see the sunlight shimmering on his outstretched and tremulous wings as he sailed round the entrance into the next valley. Weyland said nothing. Mr. Brown was silent. But as we once more moved on, the Member for Bourton-in-the-Marsh, apparently grown reckless, began to hum carelessly, "A life on the Ocean Wave."

"I wish you'd stop that row, and give other people a chance, if you can't shoot yourself," said Weyland, half in joke and half in irritated earnest.

"At all events," said Mr. Brown, stopping short and drawing himself up, "at all events, I expected to go shooting with gentlemen."

"Gentlemen be hanged!" said the Member for

Slow; and at the same moment one of the setters came upon a small pack of fine birds. The other setter creeping forward a little too jealously, the birds sprang up. Four of them fell; the fifth went straight past Mr. Brown, at a distance of about thirty-five yards, and sailed across the valley to the opposite mountain.

"Why didn't you fire?" asked Weyland of Mr. Brown, when the retriever had brought back one of the birds that had only been winged.

Mr. Brown did not answer. He glanced carelessly round, as if admiring the warm tints of the hills, and the effect of the sunlight on the rocks and heather. Then he said, with a slight air of contempt,—

"I do not see the attractions of a sport that is marked by indiscriminate slaughter, and by a good deal of ill-temper. I do not desire to be proficient in it. I can dispense with the fame of being an accomplished butcher of harmless birds. You may think it fine to kill grouse in that fashion; but I would as soon shoot pigeons at Hurlingham."

"Shoot at them, you mean," said Mr. Weyland, cruelly; and then the Member for Slow went over to his friend, and pacified him, and apologized to him, and got him into a good humour. This incident took up a little time; but the fact was that the terrible heat which was now beating down made such stoppages far from ungrateful. Even Donald, the gillie, remarked with a sigh, as he mopped his face with his weather-beaten bonnet, "It iss a most terriple warm tay, as ever wass seen." The *redintegratio amoris* between the two faithful friends who had fallen out was marked by the passing round of a flask of Lagavulin, and again we urged on our wild career.

Certainly, there was no lack of sport. The birds were plentiful, far from wild, and we were lucky enough to get the packs well broken up, and odd birds scored down, before attacking new districts. But Mr. Brown never recovered from the demoralization of his first mistakes. After failing altogether to fire at one or two birds that offered him easy shots, he was counselled to wake up his spirits by a dose of that mellow liquid which had its origin in the island lying over there in the blue sea. It is to be feared that the Member for Bourton-in-the-Marsh took the advice too much to heart, or it may have been that the Lagavulin had an unusual effect on a system weakened by the extreme heat, by disappointment, and despair. Mr. Brown, M.P., took two deep draughts from his own particular flask, and thereupon declared that the day was but young yet. He had made some blunders, doubtless; but his hand was out. He said there was nothing more beautiful than to see a setter work the side of a hill in the stillness of the midday sun.

Mr. Brown had just made this remark—in an unnecessarily loud voice—when, some distance ahead, a large black cock got up with a prodigious clatter, and betook himself to the heights above. Mr. Brown jumped, but did not put up his gun. "Well done!" said Weyland, approvingly. Alas! the very next moment there rose a grey hen, and Mr. Brown, being deceived by the colour, fired hastily. What was our astonishment to see the bird—which was certainly fifty yards off—drop like a stone! When Mr. Brown was told what he had done, he took no more shame to himself. He snapped his fingers, and uttered a fiendish laugh.

"Black cock, white cock," he said, gaily, "red grouse or grey grouse, ptarmigan, snipe, capercailzie, or stags a hundred feet high, I'll kill 'em all —I'll kill 'em all!"

The Member for Slow regarded his friend with a stupified air.

"Come along," said Mr. Brown lightly. "What's the use of drawing fine distinctions? We're outraging all humanitarian notions in making the killing of birds an amusement, and we may as well go in for unbridled licence. What can a few days matter to a black cock? Come along—let's have plenty of shooting—at anything! Wake 'em up, old MacPhairson, or MacDuncan, or whatever they call you. Ha!"

And bang went Mr. Brown's gun at a fine cock

grouse which his loud talking had put up almost out of range. Yet again the reckless Member of Parliament brought down his quarry; and again he uttered a wild laugh of triumph.

"You can't deny that's a grouse, can you?" he exclaimed, fiercely thrusting in another cartridge. "Forward, you chieftain of the clan MacGillie Callum! I will slay every wild animal in the island of Jura before I have done with you."

The success of Mr. Brown was truly surprising; but it was not to be wondered at that no one else got a shot. His jubilant cries and his urging on of the dogs—in spite of the angry expostulations of Mr. Weyland, and the plaintive remonstrances of the gillie—put up the birds at extraordinary distances, while his luck in firing recklessly at them was marvellous. The more disgusted his companions were, the more wildly Mr. Brown laughed, until we wondered what demon out of *Der Freischütz* had transformed the ordinarily quiet and amiable Member for Bourton-in-the-Marsh. At last he flung himself down on the heather, placed his gun beside him, and waved his cap over his head.

"How many have I killed, slain, mangled, and extirpated? A hundred brace, if I have touched a feather! And you say I can't shoot, you counter-jumpers, who can't touch a bird unless you're near enough to put salt on his tail. I'll tell you what I'll do with you, merely to give you a chance. I shall stop here and smoke a cigar for an hour or so, and you can come back this way. Donald, Dougal, Duncan, or Alexander Mac-Tavish, you leave those hordes of slain here, and go on with the dogs!"

When we returned that way, some two hours thereafter, Mr. Brown, M.P., was fast asleep on the hill-side, his cap over his face, and his head surrounded by a halo of killed grouse, that were lying in picturesque groups on the heather. He awoke with an air of bewildered surprise, but assented eagerly to our proposal that—in view of the excessive and insufferable heat—we should give up shooting for the day, and return to the Kittiwake for luncheon. Very proudly did he march down the glen; and as we sat in the stern of the Kittiwake that afternoon, and talked of his day's performances, Mr. Brown, M.P., took a cigar from his mouth, and airily offered to shoot grouse, for a bet, against any man in or out of the Hebrides.

CHAPTER XII.

AMONG THE MOUNTAIN HARES.

"This," said Mr. Brown, M.P., "is enjoyment."

We had gone ashore after dinner, and wandered along the rough coast-road in the falling twilight. Mr. Brown was now seated on a huge boulder of rock, out at a promontory that jutted into the sea, and, as he calmly smoked his cigar, he listened to the sound of the waves around him, as they plashed on the stony beach. In the cold green light that filled the sky the stars were not yet visible; but the darkness was sufficient to show us certain glittering orange points along the opposite shores of Islay, where the lights of Port-Ascaig burned yellow in the dusk. The air was filled with the odour of the seaweed. As the darkness deepened we heard the calling of the sea-birds far out at sea; and the islands of Colonsay and Oronsay, that had lain like masses of cloud along the horizon, now wholly disappeared. There was no sign of life around us but the green and red lights of the Kittiwake, that sent two quivering lines of colour down on the moving plain.

"Here," said Mr. Brown, in an absent way, "we can think of something better than killing harmless deer and slaughtering frightened birds. We forget the stupid and boorish exhilaration of the chase, and seek the calm and pensive contemplation of the sea. Do you think that any man could live by the sea, and fail to be a poet? Look at it now—listen to the distant calling of the waves, as if they were holding some wild Walpurgis night out there in the darkness. If I had lived on the shores of Crinan, like Campbell, I, too, might have written something like that splendid sea-song which is the only national hymn worthy of the name that we have got; and who could dwell among these lonely islands without imagining such visionary stories and legends as that of the Maid of Colonsay? What is the beginning of it?—

> On Jura's heath how sweetly swell
>   The murmurs of the mountain bee!
> How softly mourns the writhèd shell
>   Of Jura's shore, its parent sea!
>
> But softer floating o'er the deep,
>   The mermaid's sweet sea-soothing lay,
> That charmed the dancing waves to sleep
>   Before the barque of Colonsay!

Don't you think there is the sound of the sea in it—the melancholy and monotonous falling of waves on the shore? But we who have our duties elsewhere—we who are driven to dwell on Factory Bills, and Militia Bills, and Gas and Water Bills, and Bills for the repression of ruffianism at elections—we who are cooped up in the hottest weather in that hushed and gloomy chamber, with the lights in the roof making all our faces of the colour of faded butter—what chance have we of walking by the shore, and having our brain filled with dreams, and constructing some wild adventure with a mermaid, or a banshee, or some such unholy and mystic daughter of Heth?"

The Member for Slow struck a vesuvian on the rock, and Mr. Brown gave a violent start. Then he said in a peevish tone—

"Of course, you want suitable companions with you, even to enjoy a brief glimpse of the sea. There are some men who care for nothing but eating, drinking, and killing other animals——"

"Meaning me," remarked the Member for Slow.

This excess of humility on the part of Mr. Weyland suddenly disarmed the Member for Bourton-in-the-Marsh. Mr. Brown protested that he had been misunderstood. He did not seek to condemn the sports of the field, in moderation. As for Weyland himself, he was one of the very pleasantest companions, said Mr. Brown, a man could meet; and how could we be sufficiently indebted to him for his hospitality?

"All right, old boy," said Weyland, "but you

are indebted to Hulishtaveg, not to me; he has given you a couple of days' excellent deer-shooting; and the gillie told me that the district we shot over to-day is the best piece of grouse-shooting Maclean has got."

"Grouse-shooting," observed Mr. Brown, with the tone of a connoisseur, "is neither so noble nor so picturesque a pastime as the shooting of red-deer. When we were to-day pottering about the hill-sides up there, I was longing to catch even a glimpse of the lofty and desolate region in which we shot the deer yesterday. But doubtless it was miles away; or perhaps a single chain of those splendid hills removed it, as it were, into another world."

At this moment we heard a voice calling out of the darkness, and, having answered the summons, there came down towards us the tall figure of Donald.

"I will pring you a message from Mester Maclean, and he wass sayin if you would like to go and shoot sa hares sa morn's mornin'. We hef a good many hares where it will not frighten either sa deer or sa grouse, and he says you are ferry welcome."

Mr. Brown, M.P., turned round on his pinnacle of rock.

"Donald," he said, "you will inform Mr. Maclean that we do not know how to thank him for his kindness; that we accept his invitation with gratitude; and that we shall meet you at a reasonable and decent hour to-morrow morning—say nine o'clock—at any point to which you may bring the dogs."

"Sa tawgs?" said Donald, in a stupified way, "what wass you wantin' tawgs for?"

"My good man," replied Mr. Brown, with gracious condescension, "Providence not having gifted us English people with the nose of a setter or pointer, how do you expect us to seek out hares on the side of a Highland hill?"

Here, however, Mr. Weyland interfered, and endeavoured to save Mr. Brown's reputation for sanity by treating the whole matter as a joke.

Donald was asked to meet us next morning; and then we returned to the yacht.

Next day we were again favoured with clear and beautiful weather, and there was a slight breeze coming in from the sea, which promised to make the climbing of the hills less broiling work than it had proved the day before. Mr. Brown had sat up till twelve on the previous night to make an abundance of cartridges, so that his pockets, as well as his belt, were liberally provided. He had formed an idea that we should have a good deal of shooting.

"Not that I consider hare-shooting an exciting thing," as we left the shore-road and began to climb up a rocky path leading by a small cottage. "Hare-shooting I look upon as the tamest of field sports. You probe up an unfortunate animal from a tuft of grass, it runs straight before you, and never dodges, and who but the merest tyro could miss it?"

"Did you ever shoot blue hares?" said Mr. Weyland.

"No, nor pink rhinoceroses," said Mr. Brown, contemptuously; for he evidently did not believe in the existence of blue hares.

By the time, however, that we reached the foot of the hill where Donald and a boy, both armed with long saugh rods, were waiting for us, Mr. Weyland had delivered such a lecture on the habits and characteristics of the *lepus variabilis* that Mr. Brown was prepared to find it green as well as blue. Indeed, when he fully understood that he was about to engage in the pursuit of a wild mountain creature his face became more grave. Was this the hare, he asked, that turned white in the winter, and lived in the region of ptarmigan, Arctic bears, and perpetual snow?

We began to ascend. Our course, in the first instance, lay up the side of a little ravine, down which a brown stream was prattling lightly; and then we got up on the first shoulder of the hill. Here a brace of black game got up, but Mr. Brown showed admirable steadiness, and allowed them to sail away unharmed to some distant place of safety. Donald and his assistant still walked on.

"Hadn't we better try this piece of swamp?" said my friend, who was apparently rather hot and considerably blown.

"It iss no use," said Donald carelessly. "Sa hares in sa goot tays keep up sa hill."

He had scarcely spoken when Mr. Brown uttered a terrific shout. Some forty yards ahead of us a hare had got up from behind a tuft of rushes; and just as we caught sight of her, Weyland had put up his gun. The next second the hare had rolled twice over on the spongy ground, and lay there.

"It wass a goot shot," said Donald gravely; "it wass as ferry goot a shot as I will have seen for many a tay."

Mr. Brown walked briskly up to the boy, who was now running back with the prize.

"*That* isn't a blue hare, any way," he remarked confidently.

"But it is," said Weyland, "and nothing else."

"Oh, very well," replied my friend; "if you like to call a dark-grey hare a blue hare, you need stop at nothing. Outside the slang of sporting men, blue is blue, and grey is grey; but if in shooting grey is blue, and blue is grey, why don't you talk of green deer and orange snipe? If this is the wonderful prodigy we have come to shoot, I don't anticipate much difficulty. As far as I can make out, it goes on four legs just like an ordinary hare; and indeed is so uncommonly like an ordinary hare that a charge of No. 6 shot won't find out the difference."

Mr. Brown smiled complacently with the air of having said a good thing, and then we set to work to gain the second shoulder of the hill. Here some greater caution was observed; and, indeed, we had just put our heads over the crest of the ascent when Donald signalled to Mr. Brown to come near him. The Member for Bourton-in-the-Marsh took his gun down from his shoulder, and, grasping it with both hands, crept forward, Donald pointed to a thick tuft of dried grass that stood by the edge of one of those long black drains that have now been cut through so many of the mountainous sheep-pastures of Scotland. From our point of view nothing was visible behind the yellow tuft of grass, but, as Donald was evidently anxious to let Mr. Brown get a shot, we waited to see him advance. What was our astonishment to see our friend suddenly put up his gun to his shoulder and fire. Nothing had stirred. We saw Mr. Brown rush forward, and then, with a triumphant gesture, he held up some dark object in the air.

"Look here, Donald," said the Member for Slow, with perceptible irritation in his voice. "Why didn't you stop him? When a man is such a fool as to shoot a hare sitting in her form, why on earth didn't you stop him?"

"Cash pless me!" said Donald, in a wondering way, "I tit not know he wass goin' to fire."

"This is rather too bad, you know, Brown," said Weyland, with ill-concealed disgust, when the Member for Bourton-in-the-Marsh came back to us.

"What is too bad?" said Mr. Brown indignantly. "Shooting a hare, when you get the opportunity? You think I ought to have let her run and then shot her? Admirable logic! What does the hare care for that few yards' scamper, and an extra minute of life? Giving her a chance for her life! Why, what a childish superstition that is, as if there were a bargain between you and the hare, or as if the hare appreciated your courtesy. Let me remind you, my dear friend, that all these fantastic notions are of modern and spurious growth. Our ancestors shot how, when, and where they could; and none of them thought of setting birds into the air to have a chance of winging a dozen of 'em. No; they shot them fairly and completely on the ground, and ate them afterwards. You, yourself, when you steal up to a stag, do you force it into the air before you fire at it? Clear your mind of cant, Weyland. For my part I put aside these ridiculous theories and superstitions—the sham metaphysics of the sporting parson!"

Here Mr. Brown took a drink, and we went on.

The noise of the shot had startled a flock of the pretty little Highland sheep that had been quietly feeding at the further end of this plateau, and a stampede had taken place, the nimble little animals trotting lightly along the bare eminences and down rocky gullies with a singular speed. Now they stood at different points and looked back, looking very picturesque with their small black heads, their curled horns, and big, intelligent eyes. We traversed the whole extent of this plateau without finding anything (a small pack of grouse got up out of shot), and then we betook ourselves to still higher ground.

Here the ascent was very rugged; masses of grey rock, with an occasional white vein of quartz glimmering in it, stood out from the side of the hill, and seemed to bar all progress. But it was here that our day's shooting properly began; and in something less than half an hour we had picked off three hares that were scuttling away among the rocks as we cautiously ascended. None of these had fallen to Mr. Brown's gun; indeed, he was too busy climbing to think of firing; and when we had reached the top of the rocks he proposed we should rest awhile, and have some brief snatch of luncheon, which Donald carried. The five hares were unslung from the stick and laid on the heather; the sandwiches were brought forth, and Mr. Brown produced his flask.

It was excessively hot. The slight breeze from the sea had died down—there was not enough left to stir the slow column of blue smoke ascending from the bowl of Mr. Brown's meerschaum. The sun seemed to scorch the close grass and heather on the rounded shoulders of the hill, and the rocks seemed as if they would splinter in the fierce heat. In the silence that succeeded luncheon we could hear only the bleating of the sheep far below us, and the distant trickling of the burn. It is probable, indeed, that sleep would have overtaken the whole party had not Mr. Brown been seen to grasp his gun stealthily. We turned. The next moment we saw him level the weapon at a hare which had just then caught sight of us and was darting up towards the rocks above. Bang! went the first barrel; a cloud of smoke rose from a piece of rock some two yards behind the hare. Bang! went the second barrel, and Mr. Brown, gazing eagerly through the smoke, found that he had actually killed his quarry. "Well shot!" called out Mr. Weyland; and then the Member for Bourton-in-the-Marsh laid down his gun quietly, and said, with a splendid affectation of indifference, "Boy, go and fetch that hare."

He took up his pipe again and smoked on peacefully.

"It was a remarkably good shot," said Mr. Weyland.

"Oh, passable," replied our friend.

"How did you catch sight of him in time?"

"I don't generally sleep in the middle of the day," said Mr. Brown, adding in a minute or two, "I am not ashamed to confess that I am rather pleased to have shot this hare. We have now two each; and I have learned that the speed of the mountain hare is not quite a synonyme for lightning."

"You underrate your skill," said Weyland, good-naturedly. "That hare just now was going an uncommonly good pace."

"Oh, all you have to do is to aim well forward —well forward," remarked Mr. Brown, seriously. "There is nothing I hate so much as to see a hare or a rabbit shot in the hind legs—it is so very unsportsmanlike. With a little practice, you know, I think I could pick up my old knack of quick shooting. Ah! you ought to have been with the shooting-parties in the Black Forest that I used to go down to from Heidelberg in my student-days. There you have to keep your wits about you, when you've got to tell between the bucks and the does as they go past you like lightning. By the way, did you ever hear 'Im Wald und auf der Haide'?"

The Member for Slow said he had not; whereupon our friend promised to sing it for us that night. And he was as good as his word. When, after the day's shooting—we only got two more hares during the whole of the afternoon—we sat down to dinner, Mr. Brown described to Hulishtaveg, in the most vivacious manner, the picturesque shooting-parties of the Prince von Fürstenberg, and then in the course of the evening he not only sung us " Im Wald und auf der Haide," but also, in tremulous and sentimental tones, the old and sad story of the " Zerbrochene Ringlein." Mr. Brown was now fairly in the land of poetry and romance. He forgot all about the Customs Clerks' grievances. He appealed to Mr. Maclean to say whether that song of the broken ring was not fit to move a whole nation to tears, and Hulishtaveg replied gravely,

" Oh, it iss a ferry goot song—a ferry goot song, whatever. And sa words o't will pe ferry like sa Gallic—oh, ferry like sa Gallic, mirover. And I trink your ferry goot health, Mester Prown, and hope you will often come again to sa Jura Hills."

CHAPTER XIII.

MR. BROWN, M.P., AT A HIGHLAND WEDDING.

ONCE more the stately Kittiwake spread forth her white wings to the breeze, and, like the seabird that she was, made out for the sea. Maclean, of Hulishtaveg, stood on the beach, and waved his bonnet in adieu—the sunlight showing us his white hair and stalwart form defined against the dark shadow of a rock.

"Farewell, brave son of the hills," said Mr. Brown, M.P., holding on by the rattlings, and talking in a mock-heroic tone, which had nevertheless something of tenderness and truth in it; "farewell, thou venerable and kindly patriarch, whose frame has the strength and the dignity of thy native mountains; whose hair is as white as the mist that hangs around them; whose nature is as warm and as genial as the sunshine that now falls over this blue sea. Think of him, Weyland, living in this lonely island, without a relative left him in the world, passing the long and dreary winters in-doors by himself, having never mixed in the crowded cities of the south, and yet bearing himself towards his servants, towards his associates, and towards strangers with the courtesy, and grace, and dignity of a perfect gentleman. And I wish there were more such gentlemen as he among our aristocracy, and that our House of Lords could show on its benches a dozen men as good as old Hulishtaveg!"

"I wish you'd let the House of Lords alone," said Mr. Weyland, sharply.

"I don't wonder you are anxious to shield them from criticism," said the Member for Bourton-in-the-Marsh, with a splendid air of contempt—"the ridiculous old nincompoops. I suppose they're sitting out on their lawns just now, in easy chairs, wheezing asthmatically in the sunshine, listening to other people shooting in their fields, and feebly endeavouring to sip beef tea."

"I presume you are not troubled with many lords among your relatives, or you'd know more about 'em," remarked the Member for Slow, with anger gathering in his eyes.

Mr. Brown laughed gaily.

"My name," he said, "is a right good old Saxon one. There were Browns in this country before ever a Norman thief set his foot on our shores, and there will be Browns in this country when the effigy of the last of the barons shall have been carted up to Madame Tussaud's, and the skeleton of the last duke placed in the British Museum among the Megatheria! Allay your wrath, Weyland. Brown is a good name. The first man who wore it earned it because he was, in actual point of fact, brown; but the first man who was called duke was probably an imbecile courtier no more fit to lead an army than to cook a beefsteak."

"It appears to me," remarked Mr. Weyland, slowly, "that you have had your head turned by the sight of the stag's horns that Maclean sent down. I don't mean to answer you according to your folly. The House of Lords is the most firmly fixed institution in the country; and I don't suppose the axis of the earth will be altered by the scraping of a mouse."

"'Gree, bairns, 'gree!" said the Glasgow bailie, "it is jist by ordinar to hear twa raisonable crayturs argy-bargying like that on a braw, fine mornin' when they micht as weel be lookin' aboot and enjoyin' theirsels. Hoose o' Loards! Bless me—what's the Hoose o' Loards to a man that's up in the Soond o' Jura! On a day like this, I wauldna fash my thoomb for twenty Hooses of Loards!"

No living man had ever before heard the bailie make so long a speech. He instantly relapsed into silence, and, having fixed on his spectacles, betook himself to his newspaper. Weyland busied himself with the tiller, and kept his eye directed towards the small harbour of Port-Ascaig, for which we were bound. The Member for Bourton-in-the-Marsh lit a cigar, went up to the bow, and proceeded lazily to scan the prospect before him—the far stretch of white sea away to the south, where Gigha (pronounced Yeea) and Cantire lay blue in the haze. And then the Kittiwake glided into the small bay, the pinnace was brought round, and in a few minutes we were on the shores of Islay. The bailie had remained behind. He was opposed to violent exercise, and so, instead of joining us in a ride across the island to meet the Kittiwake in Loch-indaal, he preferred to make the full circuit with the yacht.

It was with some difficulty that we procured the three animals we required to take us across, and there was even more trouble about getting the necessary harness. In our quest we were much helped by the ferryman who runs a small boat between Port-Ascaig and Jura. At last the steeds were forthcoming; and very sorry-looking creatures they were—rough raw-boned brutes, that looked melancholy for want of the familiar cart-shafts, and yet allowed us to mount with a docile resignation that was almost pathetic. Indeed, what with Weyland's yachting costume of blue and brass buttons, and

Mr. Brown's suit of light grey tartan, completed with a Glengarry cap and a cigar, it is to be feared that our procession—as we left the small and thoroughly astonished village—was more remarkable for variety and picturesqueness than for any deference to the customs of civilized life; and Mr. Brown, as he gently entreated his charger to ascend the hill lying behind Port-Ascaig, could not forbear speculating on the reception which would have been accorded to us in Hyde-park on some pleasant forenoon in July. But the quiet and simple Highland folk about saw nothing peculiar in our appearance; and the ferryman aforesaid, on our leaving, hinted that we were probably going over to the marriage at Bridge-end.

"What marriage?" said Mr. Brown.

"Oh, it will pe shist sa marriage o' John Mac-Dougal, sa tailor frae Greenock, wi sa tochter o' Sligan-dubh. Sey are koin to pe married at sa inn."

"Why, the very inn we proposed to stay at," remarked Mr. Brown, in alarm; "and I suppose it will be filled with the whole clan MacDougal, including a dozen pipers."

We did not desist from our project, however; and in course of time we found ourselves up amid the lonely flats of Islay, with the air around us filled with the resinous odour of the sweet-gale, the most fragrant of all the marsh-plants. The three horses we had borrowed were not subjected to a severe pace; on the contrary, they were allowed to walk so leisurely for the most part of the journey that we found it more convenient and more pleasant to descend and lead them. By this time the two members of Parliament had made up the brief quarrel of the morning; and Mr. Brown was engaged in detailing to his friend such of the grievances of the Customs clerks as he had already been made familiar with. His study of the documents had been postponed by unavoidable causes; but he had nevertheless a vague notion of the subject, and perhaps satisfied his conscience by talking of what he knew. There was not much else to attract attention. The interior of Islay is far from being as picturesque as Jura. It consists chiefly of undulating moorland, here and there broken up by the bed of a stream, and showing an occasional cottage or farm-house, the fields surrounding which stretch out into the black and unclaimed morass. The road was most desolate. Scarcely a human being was to be seen for miles. But at last we beheld a wondrous sight in this solitude—a long string of people, in gay dresses, coming up the road in pairs, and preceded by two pipers. And while they were yet distant we heard the strange, wild music of the pipes, that had something in its peculiar wail and skirl that seemed appropriate to this savage wilderness. As we drew nearer the music resolved itself into an air, and we knew that this was the wedding-party, for the pipes were playing no pibroch of Locheil, but the familiar Lowland tune of " Wooed and married and a'." After the pipers came the bridegroom and bride, the former a tall young fellow, whose pale face and slight figure contrasted strongly with the browned, bearded, and thickset men who followed in the procession. The bride was a fresh and healthy-looking lass, with rosy cheeks, dark hair, and dark blue eyes, who blushed prodigiously at the jokes which were being shouted by the company. Immediately behind the wedded pair came the best-man, arm-in-arm with the chief bridesmaid, and then followed the string of friends and relatives, the old people winding up the procession.

As we got near them they turned into a house that stood a short distance from the way-side; but the best-man remained for a second or two until we came up, and insisted on our drinking the good health of the young couple. In answer to Mr. Brown's inquiries he explained that this was his house; that they were going to remain there for an hour or two before going on to the bridegroom's father's farm; that the marriage had taken place down at Bridge-end Inn, and that the tall tailor was a great favourite, for he had come a fortnight in advance of the marriage, and gone round to the houses of his friends, and presented them each with a day's sewing. The best-man pointed to his own coat and waistcoat—garments composed of thick and rough homespun cloth—as an evidence of MacDougal's skill; and added that, in return, he thought the least he could do was to send on three gallons of the best Lagavulin whisky to Mac-Dougal's father's farm.

"There will pe sa great doins there this nicht," he said. "There will pe forty or fifty folk there, and there is two fiddlers comin' ower frae Bowmore, besides sa twa pipers. It will pe a ferry goot weddin' whatever; and sa minister—he took a glass o' whusky wi us, and said that Bella was as braw a lass as he had married for years and years tagether. Wass you koin to Bridge-end or Bowmore?"

"We are going to Bridge-end," replied Mr. Brown, in a bland manner, "but we are not in any hurry; and if you would be kind enough to let us join your party for a short time, I should be delighted to send down to Bridge-end for another gallon of Lagavulin."

The small blue eyes in the sunburned face were opened to their fullest extent.

"What wass you sayin'? More whusky? Cash pless me, our whusky is ferry goot—oh, ferry goot whusky! What wass you wantin' to send to Bridge-end for?—but come in to sa hoose—come in to sa hoose—and you will find it ferry goot whusky whatever."

We abandoned our steeds to the care of an urchin; but, instead of going into the house, went up into the yard, whither nearly all the party had preceded us. Here two "four-some reels" were being danced with immense vigour, the piper standing firm and erect, blowing lustily, and tapping on the ground with his foot in time with the wild music. And when this performer—an old man, with long grey hair, who was the only person present wearing kilts—was marched up to the chair on which a cask of Lagavulin was placed, his post was occupied by one of the guests, who had found an old violin somewhere. Why was it that all the young folk sprang up when he began to play? Mr. Brown, M.P., snapping his fingers in time to the music, and laughing prodigiously, and crying,

"Hey!" occasionally, as some strapping young fellow gave a grand pirouette in the air, was suddenly startled by the departure of the violin into a series of discordant shrieks. Lo! the reel stopped. Each of the bearded dancers caught his partner, and, after a little rough by-play, succeeded in imprinting a kiss on her rosy and blushing cheek. And then the violin returned to its more decorous duties; the reel was recommenced; and the couples danced on until they were tired, and until the men were ready for another dram.

Mr. Brown, M.P., was subsequently introduced to the bride; but, as her stock of English was very limited, her share in the conversation chiefly consisted of blushing. The old people were very pleased to have strangers grace the ceremony; but here again there were obstacles, for all the English the bride's mother knew was, "Coot tay, sir, coot tay!" It was, however, pointed out to the Member for Bourton-in-the-Marsh that he was delaying the procession, which had yet about a dozen miles of rough moorland and bog to get over; and so, as we got on our horses again, out came the two pipers and the fiddler—all playing at once—the company once more divided itself into pairs, and away they went along the road, with many a laugh and a joke. The best-man, who was certainly excited, shook hands with us in a most affectionate manner on parting; and indeed it seemed probable that he would shed tears.

When we got down to Bridge-end Inn we found that the excitement caused by the marriage had not subsided there. Some friends from the northern side of the island, who could not go all the way, had remained in the inn, and they, too, had a piper. The marriage had been solemnised in the public-room of the place—chairs and tables having been cleared out; and in this empty room the remaining visitors were now holding high jinks—dancing, drinking, and joking, while in the corner an old man was singing, to a select audience, in a shrill, quavering key, some song which was probably of his own composition. Our host informed us that they would soon start on their homeward journey, piper and all; and so, having arranged about getting the three chargers returned to Port-Ascaig, we set off for an afternoon stroll.

Issuing from the trees round Bridge-end we came in sight of the broad waters of Loch-indaal (pronounced Loch-indawl, the accent on the last syllable), with the small town of Bowmore sending up a faint cloud of blue smoke into the evening sky. There was a stiff breeze blowing up from the west, and a small sailing-boat—probably a ferry between Bowmore and the other side of the loch— was dipping well to the waves and scattering the white foam from her bows. Of course, there were as yet no tidings of the Kittiwake; and we could only imagine her making head against the wind away on the northern side of the island, with our friend the Glasgow bailie looking out on the open waters of the Atlantic or gazing down into the south to find on the misty horizon the pale blue line of the Irish coast.

CHAPTER XIV.

HOMEWARD BOUND.

WHILE the Kittiwake lay in Loch Indaal a batch of letters arrived; and among them was one which seemed to cause Mr. Brown, M. P., some concern. By the aid of a telescope, he had been endeavouring to make out the Irish coast; but now he came aft, laid down the glass, and informed us gravely that Mr. —— had sent him an invitation to go shooting in Berkshire. Now this Mr. —— is a Cabinet Minister, and there were many reasons, said Mr. Brown, why the invitation should be at once accepted.

"I should have thought Cabinet Ministers had had enough of Berkshire," said the Member for Slow, with a sneer. "Why doesn't he ask you to go shooting in Hampshire? But, if you must go, don't be in a hurry. I will take you back to Greenock, and there you can get the London train. Besides, you know, you have to call in at Arran for your kilts."

"True," said Mr. Brown, thoughtfully. "And there is another reason why a day or two's delay might be advisable. Somehow or other I have never been able to study those papers I brought away with me, you know, referring to the grievances of the Customs clerks. Here is a capital opportunity. A day or two devoted to them will be time well spent; for then I shall go up to Berkshire with the subject fresh in my mind, and be able to lay it before ——. Indeed, I am very glad that I have so far postponed the consideration of those documents; but now there must be no further delay."

All this was satisfactory. The Kittiwake spread out her white sails, Weyland took up his post at the tiller, and very soon she was cutting through the blue plain of Loch Indaal, with a dash of curling foam at her bows, a gurgling of waters along her bulwarks, and a line of hissing white in her wake. As we got out into the open sea, we caught sight of the Rathlin Isles lying like a faint thread of purple on the southern horizon. Rounding the Mull of Islay, we got into rather a heavy sea; and not unfrequently one of the long-rolling Atlantic waves would rush up to the Kittiwake, take her at a disadvantage, and send a deluge of water over her decks. There was a brisk breeze, too, and when some less formidable wave hit the side of the yacht and rose towering into the air, the wind tossed the spray all over us, until our waterproofs gleamed wet in the sunshine.

"Is she not rather a small boat to be out in the open sea?" said Mr. Brown, timidly, looking away down towards the North Channel and the stormy Mull of Cantire.

"Why this is nothing," said the Member for Slow, shaking the salt water from his beard, " this is nothing to what you'll get going round the Mull. If you like we can run in for Port Ellen and take her up through the Crinan to-morrow; but with this wind we'll get clean away round to Arran this afternoon, and there is no more danger than if you were sitting in a hansom in Palace-yard."

"Oh, I'm not afraid," said the Member for Bourton-in-the-Marsh, standing erect, but grasping the twisted steel shrouds with a firm hand. "Don't imagine I am afraid. Personally, I like this—I enjoy it—it stirs your blood and sets your spirits on fire—but—but it was the safety of the boat I was thinking of."

"Oh, the yacht will take care of herself," said Mr. Weyland, good-naturedly. "In this sort of weather a sea-swallow is as safe as an albatross."

Certainly, the Kittiwake behaved very well, and as we got further to the south, a greater strain was put on her seafaring qualities. We were now fully exposed to the long Atlantic swell, and each time the clean little vessel went shivering down into the trough of a wave, the next great green mountain seemed looming over her, as if about to break and engulf her. How lightly she rose, with the grace of a sea-bird, to the summit of these mighty waves—how she seemed to shake the white foam back from her bows—and how she still sped southward—apparently the only living thing on this great waste of waters—cannot be described. Weyland spoke of her affectionately, as of a companion who had gone with him on many a quest, and never failed. He laughed, and talked, and joked at the pitch of his voice; while his face, grown red with the beating of the spray and gleaming with the wet, burned in the sunlight. A finer day for such an excursion could scarcely have been wished for. Overhead, the sky was a plain of deep, pure blue; and not a cloud was visible, except some white patches of mist that hung about the mountains of Jura far up in the north. Down in the south the outline of the Irish coast remained still indistinct; but the Mull of Cantire was gradually becoming more clear, and we could see a white spurt of foam occasionally springing up the face of the precipitous rocks. All around us the hurrying plain of waves showed a thousand colours, as the sunlight, and the green colour of the sea, and the blue reflection of the sky struggled for mastery, and gleamed here and there on the innumerable angles of the water. In the far distance, however, the reflection of the sky prevailed; and around the shores of Cantire the sea was of a dark, intense, and troubled blue.

It was not until we got down to the Mull that Mr. Brown, M.P., succumbed, and went below. There was some excuse for him. Here the regular swell of the Atlantic was broken up by a series of currents—they say that five tides meet just south of that wild promontory—and the result was an irregular, chopping sea, that knocked the Kittiwake about as if she were a cork. We saw no more of the member for Bourton-in-the-Marsh. He missed the sight of that strange wall of fissured rock, up which spouts of foam were leaping to a height of sixty or eighty feet as the heavy waves dashed in on the iron-bound coast. But as we got past the Sanda light-house the sea was less rough; and by the time we had got round Pladda, and into the calmer waters to leeward of the Kildonan Rocks, the Kittiwake had recovered her equanimity, and her decks were becoming dry.

Then Mr. Brown, M.P., appeared. His face was very white; but he endeavoured to assume a cheerful look.

"Yes," said he, "I have made some progress with those Customs papers now. It is astonishing what you can do in a short space of time, when you put your mind to it."

"I am glad the yacht did not pitch so as to interfere with your study," remarked Mr. Weyland, gravely.

"Well," said Mr. Brown, with a candid air, "it was rather rough, wasn't it? But I'm not such a bad sailor, you know."

Here he began to whistle "A Life on the Ocean Wave;" and by-and-by, while the colour was slowly returning to his face, we ran up by the coast of Arran, getting a glimpse of the smooth waters and string of cottages of Whiting Bay, the round shoulders of the Holy Island, and the not very picturesque houses of Lamlash, until we finally rounded Clachland Point, and stood in towards Brodick Bay, anchoring not far from the jetty used by the ferry-boats.

We landed in the pinnace, and made our way up to the hotel, where a large parcel was found waiting for Mr. Brown, M.P. He blushed slightly on being informed of the fact; Mr. Weyland laughed. The fact was that some days before Weyland had persuaded our friend to order a suit of kilts from a tailor in Glasgow, as a memento of his Highland tour. Mr. Brown was shy at first; but it was pointed out to him that at a fancy ball, or at one of the Scotch celebrations in London, his picturesque costume would stand him in good stead. At length he was persuaded; and the tailor was directed to send the bundle down to Brodick, where the Kittiwake was to call.

For a long time Mr. Brown was doubtful about those kilts. The fact was we had not seen, in all our wanderings over Highlands and Lowlands, a single Scotchman wear the traditional garb of his country, except here and there a gamekeeper and a few English tourists. But at last, the costume being ready to his hand, and Brodick being a small place in which to try the experiment, he at length retired to a dressing-room, and we lost sight of him.

When Mr. Brown, M.P., came down-stairs again our first impulse was certainly not to laugh at him. There was a mute and sensitive appeal in his eyes. Weyland spoke of the costume approvingly and in a light manner; and then hinted that Mr. Brown might accompany us down to a little wooden erection near the jetty, where we proposed to purchase some photographs. Our friend glanced rather nervously out into the open air, as little boys do when they are about to be carried down for their first dip in the sea. Then a ghastly and painful smile appeared on his face for a moment, and he said, "All right."

We went out. Mr. Brown's costume, in the tartan of the Gordons, was resplendent, and the silver mountings and flashing jewels with which it was set shone in the evening light. Unhappily, however, the most conspicuous part of him was that which the kilt left uncovered, and there Mr. Brown seemed to rival the snowy whiteness of Andromeda, as she stood chained on the rock over the blue sea. Once or twice we caught him glancing apprehensively down, and a shiver occasionally passed through his frame as the wind blew up from the bay. However, no one spoke of his dress, and he in a somewhat loud tone of voice began to say—

"What do you think, Weyland, I ought to do with that solan goose? I know a family of very nice young ladies at Laurie Park, Sydenham, and I should like to send them something from Scotland. Would the stuffed solan do? I hate sending game, which is in effect a commonplace and ridiculous custom, filling people's larders for nothing, and cheating the poulterer out of his legitimate gains. I think I shall send the deer's horns home to my own house, and the stuffed solan down to Sydenham."

There were a few loiterers about the small quay. Their eyes were apparently attracted towards Mr. Brown. He paid no attention. On the contrary he began to hum a French song—something about " *Mire dans mes yeux tes yeux, ma belle brunette* "— and then we reached the photographer's shop or hut, into which we escaped from the gaze of the vulgar.

There was a very charming young lady of about thirteen selling those sixpenny treasures of art. Mr. Brown had entered the place with something of a swagger, but now he seemed anxious to get either of his companions to stand in front of him. He even seemed to crouch down a little bit whenever the soft eyes of this amiable young person were turned towards him. His face wore an uncomfortable look. He bought things recklessly. He answered at haphazard, and in rather a snappish tone. At last, when we got out, he said, in a voice of suppressed rage:

"Why did the fool make those confounded things so short!"

"They are quite as long as usual," said Weyland, " only you're not accustomed to them."

He had scarcely uttered the words when a sudden commotion occurred. A keeper had come down to the jetty with a brace of setters in leash, and a big black retriever, with rather wolfish eyes. No sooner did the black dog behold Mr. Brown and the unusual spectacle of his milk-white calves, than he rushed furiously at him. Mr. Brown uttered a sharp, low cry, and stumbled backward into the photographer's shop. The dog followed him, closed up on him, and stood with his fore feet stuck out, barking wildly, and apparently about to spring at the members which had offended him. An exciting scene now followed. The young lady endeavoured to push back the dog with an umbrella. Mr. Brown, with a face grown white, tried to get behind the small counter, and failed. Weyland aimed a kick at the brute, and missed. The keeper tried to collar him, without avail; and it was not until a whole *posse comitatus* of boatmen, servants, and loungers had hunted the dog off and tied him up that our pale and alarmed friend ventured forth. We got him up to the hotel, where he took a little brandy, and then tried to put a brave face on the matter.

"Those horrid curs!" he exclaimed; "I wonder if that brute belongs to the Duke of Hamilton. If so I should be inclined to write to him, and I am sure the Duke would order the keeper to shoot the dog."

"You have had rather an adventure with your kilts," said the Member for Slow in a kind way.

"I shan't take them off for that," said Mr. Brown, courageously.

It was now close upon dinner-time, and we walked into the large room. One or two people were already there, and among them were a lady and her two daughters, whom Weyland knew. He took occasion to introduce his friends; and Mr. Brown found himself constrained to bring forward a chair and sit down in front of the mamma. Presently we observed that there was a crimson hue over his forehead, and he spoke in a nervous fashion.

We could see him twitching at his kilts occasionally, and edging his chair round. The colour in his face deepened; his embarrassment grew painfully obvious. At length he rose to his feet, and said, in almost an excited way—

"Will you excuse me, Madam? I think I have forgotten my—my—my handkerchief."

With that he got out of the room; and in about a quarter of an hour, when we were all at dinner, he returned, in the ordinary attire of a sane person. But rage fierce and uncontrollable still dwelt in his eyes.

"Think of the infamous ruffian," he said, in a vicious whisper, "making a costume like that, and we supposed to be living in civilized society! I declare I'll give them to the first crossing-sweeper I meet at Notting-hill, and make him wear them to bring eternal disgrace on garments that are not fit for a savage. The Caledonian Ball? Bah, I suppose the gentlemen who go to that interesting ceremony complain of the dresses worn by ballet girls. They ought to be ashamed of themselves."

"Which?" said Weyland, "the gentlemen or the ballet girls?"

"You," replied Mr. Brown, "for having inveigled me into making an ass of myself. But you don't catch me doing it again; no, never, if I lived in the desert of Sahara, without a human being to be found within a thousand miles of me. It is not, however, the ridicule of the vulgar that I fear; it is the censure of your own mind when you have been led to sacrifice your self-respect."

Mr. Brown's vehemence, however, died down; and after dinner when we were peacefully smoking a cigar, he even managed to laugh over the adventure with the dog. And then he told us in a confidential mood of the manner in which he meant to appeal to the Cabinet Minister about the grievances of the Customs clerks, and of the great deeds he expected to do among the partridges after his experiences in the North.

CHAPTER XV.

THE LAST TURN.

MR. BROWN had now to decide whether he would remain in Arran next day, and get up to Greenock on the following morning, or whether he would finish up his Highland wanderings by a run through the Kyles of Bute. He wisely chose the latter alternative. Like children on a garden-swing, he wanted "a good one for the last;" and Weyland had quite stimulated his curiosity by his talk of the fairy loveliness of the Kyles.

"Besides," said Mr. Brown, "during the quiet sail up there, I shall be able to give an hour or two to those papers. I have little time left now, and must economise it."

Accordingly, on a beautiful and bright forenoon, we bade farewell to Brodick Bay, and stood out into the broad estuary of the Clyde, which is here as spacious and as clear as an inland sea. We had a magnificent view of the Arran mountains as we got out some little distance from the shore—their splendid peaks just touched here and there with a flake of white cloud, while a flood of sunlight poured down on the great valleys of Glen Rosa and Glen Sannox, and lay drowsily on the fir-forests surrounding Brodick Castle. We passed the steamer coming over from Ardrossan; and Mr. Brown, standing at the bow, waved his handkerchief to the passengers—a salute which was returned.

It was indeed a pleasant morning. There was just enough westerly wind to fill our sails and ruffle the blue bosom of the deep; and the Kittiwake, scarcely lying over, cut lightly through the water. The further we got north, the more lovely seemed the prospect that lay all around us. Over there on the right were the smooth hills and long-stretching woods of Ayrshire, with the towns of Troon, Irvine, and Ardrossan glimmering through a faint haze of smoke; further up the two Cumbraes seemed to be almost close inshore; right ahead of us were the lonely shores and green undulations of the island of Bute; and away on our left, the Sound of Bute stretched up towards the Cowal coast and the broad mouth of Loch Fyne.

Nowhere in all our wanderings had we seen such numbers and varieties of sea-birds; and Mr. Brown's attention was wholly given up to watching for long strings of wild-duck, and clouds of tern, and clusters of guillemots floating on the waves. Great was his anxiety, too, to discover whether each white gull that appeared in the distance was not a solan; and, in point of fact, he was gratified by the sight of at least half-a-dozen of those birds—hovering singly, for the most part, over the smooth waters that lay under the shadow of the shores of Cantire. At last, so many and so various were the strange animals that kept flying about and tantalising him, that he went below and fetched up Weyland's gun.

"I thought you had gone down for the Customs

clerks' papers," remarked the Member for Slow, gravely.

"Bother the Customs clerks' papers!" said Mr. Brown; and then he added, in rather a vexed tone, "why can't you allow a man to have a moment's relaxation? No sooner does one begin to feel amused and prone to enjoy the passing moments without thinking, than you must thrust forward your admonitions about work. I don't think it's friendly. I don't see that you do so much work yourself."

Weyland looked surprised.

"Why," said he, "I never mentioned the matter before, and you have done nothing ever since you have been on board but talk of your confounded Customs clerks, and what you meant to do with them. You needn't get into a temper simply because you have been indolent."

"Indolent!" said the Member for Bourton-in-the-Marsh, laughing bitterly. "Indolent! when I escaped from the fag end of a laborious session to recruit my health, which had been broken by late hours and close attention to parliamentary business, there was not much call for me to attack new work. Yet I did it voluntarily. Of my own free will I undertook this task. Of my own free will I have devoted my leisure to the study of those papers——"

"When?" said Weyland.

"When you were asleep, as you generally are," was the retort.

At this point both members of parliament, catching each other's eye, burst out laughing; and the Scotch bailie, who had not spoken a word all the morning, joined in.

"To hear ye talk," said our stout friend, "ane would think ye had nae mair mainners than a wheen school-laddies. But I'm thinking ye have learnt a' that in Paurliament. Short o' downright sweerin', the language sometimes used on both sides o' the House is only fit for carters."

"But the Conservative side at least preserves the show of courtesy," remarked Weyland.

"The Liberal side," retorted Mr. Brown,

"having truth for its banner, can afford to speak fearlessly, and express its opinions about its opponents."

With that, the Member for Bourton-in-the-Marsh departed to the bow of the Kittiwake, with Weyland's breech-loader in his hand, and the grievances of the Customs clerks were once more relegated to the unknown future.

We were now in Inchmarnoch Water, and before us appeared the entrance into the magic wonders of the Kyles. A soft summer haze lay over the wooded hills and rocks, and the breeze was insensibly fading off; so that to leeward of Ardlamont Point the sea was still and smooth. It did not seem probable that we should get sufficient wind to carry us up to Tighnabruich; but we were still creeping along, and in course of time we were fairly up to Ardlamont Point, and into the Kyles.

Even as the discovery of America was announced by the firing of a cannon from the vessel of Fernandez Ponto, so our entrance into the Kyles of Bute was signalised by the report of Mr. Brown's breech-loader. We looked up towards the bow, and beheld our friend gesticulating wildly to the sailors, while some distance ahead a small object was floating on the water. The yacht was run close up to it, and then one of the sailors dexterously fished up the dead bird from the waves. It was a tern; and as Mr. Brown came aft in triumph, to show us the beautiful grey and speckled plumage and the curved, swallow-like wings, Weyland said—

"What a shame to kill one of those birds! It is mere wanton slaughter."

"I don't see it in that light," remarked Mr. Brown coolly. "I am going down partridge-shooting. I wished to try the distance you must fire in front of a bird going at a great speed, and so I fired at this tern as he was going past like lightning. You see the result. It was a test—the tern being nearly of the same size as the partridge."

"Is it? I suppose you mean to fire at cheepers or anything, and have ———, cabinet minister as he is, swearing at you like a trooper."

"I am not in the habit of making myself ridiculous when out shooting," said Mr. Brown, with some dignity.

But this incident of the tern seemed to have drawn our friend's attention in a new direction. He kept fidgeting about with the gun. He lamented that there would not now be time for his forming that collection of sea-birds he had once spoken of. He spoke of nothing but powder and lead, and wads and charges, until, finally, he said to Weyland, in an appealing voice—

"I say, Weyland, couldn't we have some shooting somewhere this afternoon?"

"Well, no," said the Member for Slow; "not unless you like to go out in the evening to pot those divers, and that is not a very exciting form of amusement."

"Oh, I think it is," said Mr. Brown, eagerly. "Fancy the romance of it—the calm of the evening—the lovely scenery—the anxiety of the chase: by all means let us go out."

Not a word about the Customs clerks. We

slowly sailed up into the Kyles: a slight breeze just sufficed to carry us onward; and as we got up to Kames, all the loveliness of the place spread out before us. For the moment Mr. Brown was drawn from watching the sea-birds to contemplating that beautiful picture—the winding channel of blue water, the craggy hills, the deep umbrageous woods coming down to the very margin of the sea, the occasional white cottage gleaming above the shingly beach, and here and there a yacht coming out with all her sails set from the recesses of some secret bay. So still the place was, too, in the afternoon sunlight! We could hear nothing but the ripple of the water along the side of the Kittiwake, and the calling of the wild birds. When at last we came to an anchorage at Tighnabruich, and landed, and walked up to the inn there, Mr. Brown declared he had seen no lovelier scenery anywhere in the world.

But these pleasant surroundings and the after-luncheon laziness of the afternoon did not wean him from his fell purpose. About six o'clock that night you might have seen us get into a little open sailing-boat, which had a heap of big stones lying along the bottom by way of ballast.

The owner and skipper of the craft was a sort of half boatman, half fisherman—an old weather-beaten man, with a Scotch bonnet and garments patched and mended in many places. He was silent and even morose, and went about his work as though we had "requirirt" his services, instead of having offered him a very handsome reward for the use of his boat.

However, Mr. Brown, M.P., took no heed of these things, nor did he pay any attention to Mr. Weyland's protestations against the unsportsman-like errand on which we were bent. It was his last evening in the Highlands. Perhaps he might never again have a chance of shooting at those wild creatures of the deep which had woven a spell of fascination over him. He even forgot the brief and emphatic speech he had made in the House on the destruction of the birds along our coast, when the bill to prevent that was brought in.

How lovely the Kyles looked now, with the red colours of the sunset shining over the sea and the hills, and catching the sides of the mountains up by Loch Striven! Far down in the south, too, the great plain lay still and silent, with here and there the sail of a fishing-smack glowing like a speck of crimson flame over the darkening surface of the waters. We lay in the stern of the small boat, and smoked our pipes, as she slowly got out to sea before a light breeze coming off the hills. Mr. Brown was up at the bow, his back against the mast, and his position partially concealed by the jib in front of him. He alone had brought a gun with him. Once or twice we saw him put it up to his shoulder; and then again he would drop it with some low-muttered exclamation.

There were birds about somewhere. We could hear them calling. Now and again a whirr of wings was audible in the distance; but none of the "dookers" came our way. At last, however, we saw the boatman touch Mr. Brown's arm, and point out to something floating on the waves, or rather ripples, of the sea. There were two black specks visible on that purple plain, and we could see the boat's prow slowly wearing round towards them. The more near we got, the more clearly we saw the two birds—obviously "dookers," with their shining black and white plumage and curved beak: They were paddling about, in open disregard of us, and sometimes stretching themselves up to flutter their wings. When the boat was certainly not more than fifteen yards from them, off went both of Mr. Brown's barrels with a noise which was echoed all along the solitary shores of the Kyles.

"What a beastly shame!" said Weyland.

"Run the boat to," shouted Mr. Brown to the man; "run her up; turn her head! I know I killed them—I am sure I killed them—I'll swear they're killed!"

The old brown-faced man did not take the least notice of Mr. Brown's excitement.

"They were doon before the shot reached them," he said, moodily.

Whether the birds had "ducked the shot," or whether Mr. Brown had blown them into nothingness, we saw no further traces of them; and so once more our friend resumed his post, and we drifted further down. A very few minutes sufficed to discover to the anxious eyes at the bow another dark object on the water; and this time, just as the bird was fluttering its wings, we again heard a loud bang! and the unfortunate animal turned over on the water, and lay there. Weyland ran the boat close to the prize, and Mr. Brown, leaning over the side, made a dash at the bird, and secured it. It is true, that at the same moment he had plunged his arm up to the elbow in the sea; but that did not damp the triumph with which he brought forward his quarry for our inspection. The bright eyes of the diver were still unglazed, and its smooth and clean plumage was dripping with the sea-water.

"What is the use of killing those unfortunate animals?" said Mr. Weyland once more.

"Practice," observed the Member for Bourton-in-the-Marsh. "It is a deal more difficult to hit those birds than you imagine, when you have to steady yourself against the heaving of the boat, and at the same time watch the moment they are likely to come to the top of a wave."

"And is that good practice for shooting in Berkshire?" inquired the Member for Slow.

"If you don't like it, we can land you," returned Mr. Brown.

"On the contrary," said Weyland, "I enjoy myself where I am, amazingly, especially when I have the pleasure of your society and amiable conversation. I was only thinking how those birds liked it."

"There are plenty of 'em," said Mr. Brown, with a callous indifference which showed the brutalising effect of a breech-loader.

And there were plenty of them. A few minutes thereafter, we steered right into a cluster of "dookers," and here Mr. Brown fired right and left, slipping in cartridges and letting them off so long as there was a bird visible. Out of the lot he got two—at least, we could only find two, for in the curious metallic glare now falling over the sea it was difficult to distinguish objects.

"Are you satisfied with your aimless slaughter now?" asked Weyland.

"I don't consider it aimless slaughter," retorted Mr. Brown, "when I mean to eat the birds."

"Eat them!"

"Yes, why not?"

"You'll have a taste of herring in your mouth for a month."

"The flavour of herring is not disagreeable in herring; why should it be in a bird? All you have to do is to imagine you are eating herring."

"Your philosophy won't prevent your becoming sick."

"We shall see," replied Mr. Brown.

It was now resolved that we should make for Tighnabruich once more, lest the wind should fail us; and the chances were, besides, that Mr. Brown would have some more shooting on the way. But even he was weaned away from his watch by the extraordinary appearances now around us. The sun had gone down; but there was still a glow of red and yellow in the west. The hills above Tighnabruich were a dark, intense purple, that heightened the wild clear glare of the sky above. But the most peculiar sight of all was the singular radiance that was over the water—a glow of strange greenish yellow that broke into a thousand shapes as the waves rolled on. In the dusk the metallic glare of the sea was almost painful to the eyes; and we were glad to turn from it to the pure colours above, where a pale blue was shaded with pink, where the eastern sky caught the reflection of the sunset. The hills about the Kyles grew more and more dark. The sickle of the moon rose in the south, but her radiance was as yet not strong enough to touch the waves. When we finally got back to Tighnabruich, there were stars faintly visible in the sky, and a cold night-wind coming down from the solitudes of the hills.

"To-morrow," said Mr. Brown, "I go south. If I have, in the excitement of the chase, offended you at any moment, Weyland, I am sorry for it. I leave Scotland, and all those magnificent scenes we have visited, with a deep and profound regret; and I shall often think of the splendid days we had together in the Kittiwake. But, you see, business calls me away—the hard and stern duties of the world. Do you think now I shall be able to study those Customs documents in the train, as I go up to London, to-morrow?"

"I don't know," said Weyland. "If I were you, I should leave them over until I got to Berkshire."

"I think I must," said Mr. Brown thoughtfully. "There is nothing that more clearly distinguishes the prudent man than the faculty of being able to sketch out and apportion his time, so as to keep work and play in their proper and relative positions."

THE END.

BRADBURY, EVANS, AND CO., PRINTERS, WHITEFRIARS.

BEDFORD STREET, COVENT GARDEN, LONDON.
June, 1872.

MACMILLAN & CO.'S CATALOGUE of Works in BELLES LETTRES, including Poetry, Fiction, Works on Art, Critical and Literary Essays, etc.

Allingham.—LAURENCE BLOOMFIELD IN IRELAND; or, the New Landlord. By WILLIAM ALLINGHAM. New and Cheaper Issue, with a Preface. Fcap. 8vo. cloth. 4s. 6d.

The aim of this little book is to do something, however small, towards making Ireland, yet so little known to the general British public, better understood. Several of the most important problems of life, Irish life and human life, are dealt with in their principles, according to the author's best lights. In the new Preface, the state of Ireland, with special reference to the Church measure, is discussed. "It is vital with the national character. . . . . It has something of Pope's point and Goldsmith's simplicity, touched to a more modern issue."—ATHENÆUM.

Arnold.—Works by MATTHEW ARNOLD :—

THE COMPLETE POETICAL WORKS. Vol. I. NARRATIVE AND ELEGIAC POEMS. Vol. II. DRAMATIC AND LYRIC POEMS. Extra fcap. 8vo. Price 6s. each.

The two volumes comprehend the First and Second Series of the Poems, and the New Poems. "Thyrsis is a poem of perfect delight, exquisite in grave tenderness of reminiscence, rich in breadth of western light, breathing full the spirit of gray and ancient Oxford."—SATURDAY REVIEW. *"The noblest in it is clothed in clearest words. There is no obscurity, no useless ornament: every-thing is simple, finished, and perfect."*—SCOTSMAN.

A

Arnold—*continued.*

ESSAYS IN CRITICISM. New Edition, with Additions. Extra fcap. 8vo. 6s.

The Essays in this Volume are—"*The Function of Criticism at the Present Time;*" "*The Literary Influence of Academies;*" "*Maurice de Guérin;*" "*Eugénie de Guérin;*" "*Heinrich Heine;*" "*Pagan and Mediæval;*" "*Religious Sentiment;*" "*Joubert;*" "*Spinoza and the Bible;*" "*Marcus Aurelius.*" *Both from the subjects dealt with and mode of treatment, few books are more calculated to delight, inform, and stimulate than these charming Essays.*

Bacon's Essays.—See GOLDEN TREASURY SERIES.

Baker.—(For other Works by the same author, see CATALOGUE OF TRAVELS.)

CAST UP BY THE SEA; OR, THE ADVENTURES OF NED GREY. By SIR SAMUEL BAKER, M.A., F.R.G.S., With Illustrations by HUARD. Fourth Edition. Crown 8vo. cloth gilt. 7s. 6d.

"*An admirable tale of adventure, of marvellous incidents, wild exploits, and terrible dénouements.*"—DAILY NEWS. "*A story of adventure by sea and land in the good old style.*"—PALL MALL GAZETTE.

Ballad Book.—See GOLDEN TREASURY SERIES.

Baring-Gould.—Works by S. BARING-GOULD, M.A. :—

IN EXITU ISRAEL. An Historical Novel. Two Vols. 8vo. 21s.

"*Some of its most powerful passages — and prodigiously powerful they are—are descriptions of familiar events in the earlier days of the Revolution.*"—LITERARY CHURCHMAN. "*Full of the most exciting incidents and ably portrayed characters, abounding in beautifully attractive legends, and relieved by descriptions fresh, vivid, and truth-like.*"—WESTMINSTER REVIEW.

aring-Gould—*continued.*

LEGENDS OF OLD TESTAMENT CHARACTERS, from the Talmud and other sources. Two vols. Crown 8vo. 16s. Vol. I. Adam to Abraham. Vol. II. Melchizedek to Zachariah.

Mr. Baring-Gould has here collected from the Talmud and other sources, Jewish and Mohammedan, a large number of curious and interesting legends concerning the principal characters of the Old Testament, comparing these frequently with similar legends current among many of the nations, savage and civilized, all over the world. "These volumes contain much that is very strange, and, to the ordinary English reader, very novel."—DAILY NEWS.

arker.—Works by LADY BARKER :—

"Lady Barker is an unrivalled story-teller."—GUARDIAN.

STATION LIFE IN NEW ZEALAND. New and Cheaper Edition. Crown 8vo. 3s. 6d.

These letters are the exact account of a lady's experience of the brighter and less practical side of colonization. They record the expeditions, adventures, and emergencies diversifying the daily life of the wife of a New Zealand sheep-farmer; and, as each was written while the novelty and excitement of the scenes it describes were fresh upon her, they may succeed in giving here in England an adequate impression of the delight and freedom of an existence so far removed from our own highly-wrought civilization. "We have never read a more truthful or a pleasanter little book."—ATHENÆUM.

SPRING COMEDIES. STORIES.

CONTENTS :—A Wedding Story—A Stupid Story—A Scotch Story—A Man's Story. Crown 8vo. 7s. 6d.

"Lady Barker is endowed with a rare and delicate gift for narrating stories,—she has the faculty of throwing even into her printed narrative a soft and pleasant tone, which goes far to make the reader think the subject or the matter immaterial, so long as the author will go on telling stories for his benefit."—ATHENÆUM.

STORIES ABOUT :—With Six Illustrations. Second Edition. Extra fcap. 8vo. 4s. 6d.

Barker—*continued.*

This volume contains several entertaining stories about Monkeys, Jamaica, Camp Life, Dogs, Boys, &c. "There is not a tale in the book which can fail to please children as well as their elders."
—PALL MALL GAZETTE.

A CHRISTMAS CAKE IN FOUR QUARTERS. With Illustrations by JELLICOE. Second Edition. Extra fcap. 8vo. cloth gilt. 4s. 6d.

In this little volume, Lady Barker, whose reputation as a delightful story-teller is established, narrates four pleasant stories showing how the "Great Birth-day" is kept in the "Four Quarters" of the globe,—in England, Jamaica, India, and New Zealand. The volume is illustrated by a number of well-executed cuts. "Contains just the stories that children should be told. 'Christmas Cake' is a delightful Christmas book."—GLOBE.

Bell.—ROMANCES AND MINOR POEMS. By HENRY GLASSFORD BELL. Fcap. 8vo. 6s.

"Full of life and genius."—COURT CIRCULAR.

Besant.—STUDIES IN EARLY FRENCH POETRY. By WALTER BESANT, M.A. Crown. 8vo. 8s. 6d.

A sort of impression rests on most minds that French literature begins with the "siècle de Louis Quatorze;" any previous literature being for the most part unknown or ignored. Few know anything of the enormous literary activity that began in the thirteenth century, was carried on by Rutebeuf, Marie de France, Gaston de Foix, Thibault de Champagne, and Lorris; was fostered by Charles of Orleans, by Margaret of Valois, by Francis the First; that gave a crowd of versifiers to France, enriched, strengthened, developed, and fixed the French language, and prepared the way for Corneille and for Racine. The present work aims to afford information and direction touching the early efforts of France in poetical literature. "In one moderately sized volume he has contrived to introduce us to the very best, if not to all of the early French poets."—ATHENÆUM.

Book of Golden Deeds.—See GOLDEN TREASURY SERIES.

Book of Golden Thoughts.—See GOLDEN TREASURY SERIES.

Book of Praise.—See GOLDEN TREASURY SERIES.

Brimley.—ESSAYS BY THE LATE GEORGE BRIMLEY, M.A. Edited by the Rev. W. G. CLARK, M.A. With Portrait. Cheaper Edition. Fcap. 8vo. 2s. 6d.

> George Brimley was regarded by those who knew him as "one of the finest critics of the day." The Essays contained in this volume are all more or less critical, and were contributed by the author to some of the leading periodicals of the day. The subjects are, "Tennyson's Poems," "Wordsworth's Poems," "Poetry and Criticism," "The Angel in the House," Carlyle's "Life of Sterling," "Esmond," "My Novel," "Bleak House," "Westward Ho!" Wilson's "Noctes Ambrosianæ," Comte's "Positive Philosophy." "It will," JOHN BULL says, "be a satisfaction to the admirers of sound criticism and unassuming common sense to find that the Essays of the late George Brimley have reappeared in a new and popular form. They will give a healthy stimulus to that spirit of inquiry into the real value of our literary men whose names we too often revere without sufficient investigation."

Broome.—THE STRANGER OF SERIPHOS. A Dramatic Poem. By FREDERICK NAPIER BROOME. Fcap. 8vo. 5s.

> Founded on the Greek legend of Danaë and Perseus. "Grace and beauty of expression are Mr. Broome's characteristics; and these qualities are displayed in many passages."—ATHENÆUM. "The story is rendered with consummate beauty."—LITERARY CHURCHMAN.

Bunyan's Pilgrim's Progress.—See GOLDEN TREASURY SERIES.

Burke.—EDMUND BURKE, a Historical Study. By JOHN MORLEY, B.A., Oxon. Crown 8vo. 7s. 6d.

> "The style is terse and incisive, and brilliant with epigram and point. Its sustained power of reasoning, its wide sweep of observation and reflection, its elevated ethical and social tone, stamp it as

a work of high excellence."—SATURDAY REVIEW. "*A model of compact condensation. We have seldom met with a book in which so much matter was compressed into so limited a space.*"—PALL MALL GAZETTE. "*An essay of unusual effort.*"—WESTMINSTER REVIEW.

Burns' Works.—See GOLDEN TREASURY SERIES and GLOBE LIBRARY.

Carroll.—Works by "LEWIS CARROLL:"—

ALICE'S ADVENTURES IN WONDERLAND. With Forty-two Illustrations by TENNIEL. 33rd Thousand. Crown 8vo. cloth. 6s.

A GERMAN TRANSLATION OF THE SAME. With TENNIEL'S Illustrations. Crown 8vo. gilt. 6s.

A FRENCH TRANSLATION OF THE SAME. With TENNIEL'S Illustrations. Crown 8vo. gilt. 6s.

AN ITALIAN TRANSLATION OF THE SAME. By T. P. ROSSETTE. With TENNIEL'S Illustrations. Crown 8vo. 6s.

"*Beyond question supreme among modern books for children.*"—SPECTATOR. "*One of the choicest and most charming books ever composed for a child's reading.*"—PALL MALL GAZETTE. "*A very pretty and highly original book, sure to delight the little world of wondering minds, and which may well please those who have unfortunately passed the years of wondering.*"—TIMES.

THROUGH THE LOOKING-GLASS, AND WHAT ALICE FOUND THERE. With Fifty Illustrations by TENNIEL. Crown 8vo. 6s. 23rd Thousand.

In the present volume is described, with inimitably clever and laughter-moving nonsense, the further Adventures of the fairy-favoured Alice, in the grotesque world which she found to exist on the other side of her mother's drawing-room looking-glass, through which she managed to make her way. The work is profusely embellished with illustrations by Tenniel, exhibiting as great an amount of humour as those to which "Alice's Adventures in Wonderland" owed so much of its popularity.

Carroll—*continued.*

PHANTASMAGORIA, AND OTHER POEMS. Fcap. 8vo. gilt edges. 6s.

> "*Those who have not made acquaintance with these poems already have a pleasure to come. The comical is so comical, and the grave so really beautiful.*"—LITERARY CHURCHMAN.

Chatterton : A BIOGRAPHICAL STUDY. By DANIEL WILSON, LL.D., Professor of History and English Literature in University College, Toronto. Crown 8vo. 6s. 6d.

> *The author here regards Chatterton as a Poet, not as a "mere reseller and defacer of stolen literary treasures." Reviewed in this light, he has found much in the old materials capable of being turned to new account : and to these materials research in various directions has enabled him to make some additions. He believes that the boy-poet has been misjudged, and that the biographies hitherto written of him are not only imperfect but untrue. While dealing tenderly, the author has sought to deal truthfully with the failings as well as the virtues of the boy : bearing always in remembrance, what has been too frequently lost sight of, that he was but a boy ;—a boy, and yet a poet of rare power. The* EXAMINER *thinks this "the most complete and the purest biography of the poet which has yet appeared."*

Children's Garland from the Best Poets.—See GOLDEN TREASURY SERIES.

Church (A. J.)—HORÆ TENNYSONIANÆ, Sive Eclogæ e Tennysono Latine redditæ. Cura A. J. CHURCH, A.M. Extra fcap. 8vo. 6s.

> *Latin versions of Selections from Tennyson. Among the authors are the Editor, the late Professor Conington, Professor Seeley, Dr. Hessey, Mr. Kebbel, and other gentlemen. "Of Mr. Church's ode we may speak in almost unqualified praise, and the same may be said of the contributions generally."*—PALL MALL GAZETTE.

Clough (Arthur Hugh).—THE POEMS AND PROSE REMAINS OF ARTHUR HUGH CLOUGH. With a

Clough (Arthur Hugh)—*continued.*

Selection from his Letters and a Memoir. Edited by his Wife. With Portrait. Two Vols. Crown 8vo. 21s. Or Poems separately, as below.

The late Professor Clough is well known as a graceful, tender poet, and as the scholarly translator of Plutarch. The letters possess high interest, not biographical only, but literary—discussing, as they do, the most important questions of the time, always in a genial spirit. The "Remains" include papers on "Retrenchment at Oxford;" on Professor F. W. Newman's book, "The Soul;" on Wordsworth; on the Formation of Classical English; on some Modern Poems (Matthew Arnold and the late Alexander Smith), &c. &c. "Taken as a whole," the SPECTATOR *says, "these volumes cannot fail to be a lasting monument of one of the most original men of our age." "Full of charming letters from Rome,"* says the MORNING STAR, *"from Greece, from America, from Oxford, and from Rugby."*

THE POEMS OF ARTHUR HUGH CLOUGH, sometime Fellow of Oriel College, Oxford. Third Edition. Fcap. 8vo. 6s.

"From the higher mind of cultivated, all-questioning, but still conservative England, in this our puzzled generation, we do not know of any utterance in literature so characteristic as the poems of Arthur Hugh Clough."—FRASER'S MAGAZINE.

Clunes.—THE STORY OF PAULINE: an Autobiography. By G. C. CLUNES. Crown 8vo. 6s.

"Both for vivid delineation of character and fluent lucidity of style, 'The Story of Pauline' is in the first rank of modern fiction."—GLOBE. *"Told with delightful vivacity, thorough appreciation of life, and a complete knowledge of character."*—MANCHESTER EXAMINER.

Collects of the Church of England. With a beautifully Coloured Floral Design to each Collect, and Illuminated Cover. Crown 8vo. 12s. Also kept in various styles of morocco.

In this richly embellished edition of the Church Collects, the paper is thick and handsome and the type large and beautiful, each Collect, with a few exceptions, being printed on a separate page. The dis-

tinctive characteristic of this edition is the floral design which accompanies each Collect, and which is generally emblematical of the character of the day or saint to which it is assigned; the flowers which have been selected are such as are likely to be in bloom on the day to which the Collect belongs. Each flower is richly but tastefully and naturally printed in colours, and from the variety of plants selected and the faithfulness of the illustrations to nature, the volume should form an instructive and interesting companion to all devout Christians, who are likely to find their devotions assisted and guided by having thus brought before them the flowers in their seasons, God's beautiful and never-failing gifts to men. The Preface explains the allusion in the case of all those illustrations which are intended to be emblematical of the days to which they belong, and the Table of Contents forms a complete botanical index, giving both the popular and scientific name of each plant. There are at least one hundred separate plants figured. "This is beyond question," the ART JOURNAL says, "the most beautiful book of the season." "Carefully, indeed lovingly drawn and daintily coloured," says the PALL MALL GAZETTE. The GUARDIAN thinks it "a successful attempt to associate in a natural and unforced manner the flowers of our fields and gardens with the course of the Christian year."

Cowper's Poetical Works.—See GLOBE LIBRARY.

Cox.—RECOLLECTIONS OF OXFORD. By G. V. COX, M.A., late Esquire Bedel and Coroner in the University of Oxford. Second and cheaper Edition. Crown 8vo. 6s.

Mr. Cox's Recollections date from the end of last century to quite recent times. They are full of old stories and traditions, epigrams and personal traits of the distinguished men who have been at Oxford during that period. The TIMES *says that it "will pleasantly recall in many a country parsonage the memory of youthful days."*

Dante.—DANTE'S COMEDY, THE HELL. Translated by W. M. ROSSETTI. Fcap. 8vo. cloth. 5s.

"The aim of this translation of Dante may be summed up in one word—Literality. To follow Dante sentence for sentence, line for line, word for word—neither more nor less, has been my strenuous endeavour."—AUTHOR'S PREFACE.

Days of Old; STORIES FROM OLD ENGLISH HISTORY. By the Author of "Ruth and her Friends." New Edition. 18mo. cloth, gilt leaves. 3s. 6d.

> *The Contents of this interesting and instructive volume are, "Caradoc and Deva," a story of British life in the first century: "Wolfgan and the Earl; or, Power," a story of Saxon England: and "Roland," a story of the Crusaders. "Full of truthful and charming historic pictures, is everywhere vital with moral and religious principles, and is written with a brightness of description, and with a dramatic force in the representation of character, that have made, and will always make, it one of the greatest favourites with reading boys."*—NONCONFORMIST.

De Vere.—THE INFANT BRIDAL, and other Poems. By AUBREY DE VERE. Fcap. 8vo. 7s. 6d.

> *"Mr. De Vere has taken his place among the poets of the day. Pure and tender feeling, and that polished restraint of style which is called classical, are the charms of the volume."*—SPECTATOR.

Doyle (Sir F. H.)—Works by Sir FRANCIS HASTINGS DOYLE, Professor of Poetry in the University of Oxford:—

THE RETURN OF THE GUARDS, AND OTHER POEMS. Fcap. 8vo. 7s.

> *"Good wine needs no bush, nor good verse a preface; and Sir Francis Doyle's verses run ....*

....., delivered before the University of Oxford in 1868. Crown 8vo. 3s. 6d.

> THREE LECTURES:—(1) *Inaugural, in which the nature of Poetry is discussed;* (2) *Provincial Poetry;* (3) *Dr. Newman's "Dream of Gerontius." "Full of thoughtful discrimination and fine insight: the lecture on 'Provincial Poetry' seems to us singularly true, eloquent, and instructive."*—SPECTATOR. *"All these dissertations are marked by a scholarly spirit, delicate taste, and the discriminating powers of a trained judgment."*—DAILY NEWS.

Dryden's Poetical Works.—See GLOBE LIBRARY.

Dürer, Albrecht.—HISTORY OF THE LIFE OF ALBRECHT DÜRER, of Nürnberg. With a Translation of his Letters and Journal, and some account of his Works. By Mrs. CHARLES HEATON. Royal 8vo. bevelled boards, extra gilt. 31s. 6d.

This work contains about Thirty Illustrations, ten of which are productions by the autotype (carbon) process, and are printed in permanent tints by Messrs. Cundall and Fleming, under licence from the Autotype Company, Limited; the rest are Photographs and Woodcuts.

Estelle Russell.—By the Author of "The Private Life of Galileo." Crown 8vo. 6s.

Full of bright pictures of French life. The English family, whose fortunes form the main drift of the story, reside mostly in France, but there are also many English characters and scenes of great interest. It is certainly the work of a fresh, vigorous, and most interesting writer, with a dash of sarcastic humour which is refreshing and not too bitter. "We can send our readers to it with confidence."—SPECTATOR.

Evans.—BROTHER FABIAN'S MANUSCRIPT, AND OTHER POEMS. By SEBASTIAN EVANS. Fcap. 8vo. cloth. 6s.

"In this volume we have full assurance that he has 'the vision and the faculty divine.' . . . Clever and full of kindly humour."—GLOBE.

Fairy Book.—The Best Popular Fairy Stories. Selected and Rendered anew by the Author of "John Halifax, Gentleman." With Coloured Illustrations and Ornamental Borders by J. E. ROGERS, Author of "Ridicula Rediviva." Crown 8vo. cloth, extra gilt. 6s. (Golden Treasury Edition. 18mo. 4s. 6d.)

"A delightful selection, in a delightful external form."—SPECTATOR. *Here are reproduced in a new and charming dress many old favourites, as "Hop-o'-my-Thumb," "Cinderella," "Beauty and the Beast," "Jack the Giant-killer," "Tom Thumb," "Rumpelstilzchen," "Jack and the Bean-stalk," "Red Riding-Hood," "The Six Swans," and a great many others. "A book which will prove delightful to children all the year round."*—PALL MALL GAZETTE.

Fletcher.—THOUGHTS FROM A GIRL'S LIFE. By LUCY FLETCHER. Second Edition. Fcap. 8vo. 4s. 6d.

"*Sweet and earnest verses, especially addressed to girls, by one who can sympathise with them, and who has endeavoured to give articulate utterance to the vague aspirations after a better life of pious endeavour, which accompany the unfolding consciousness of the inner life in girlhood. The poems are all graceful; they are marked throughout by an accent of reality; the thoughts and emotions are genuine.*"—ATHENÆUM.

Freeman (E. A., Hon. D.C.L.)—HISTORICAL ESSAYS. By EDWARD FREEMAN, M.A., Hon. D.C.L., late Fellow of Trinity College, Oxford. Second Edition. 8vo. 10s. 6d.

This volume contains twelve Essays selected from the author's contributions to various Reviews. The principle on which they were chosen was that of selecting papers which referred to comparatively modern times, or, at least, to the existing states and nations of Europe. By a sort of accident a number of the pieces chosen have thrown themselves into something like a continuous series bearing on the historical causes of the great events of 1870—71. *Notes have been added whenever they seemed to be called for; and whenever he could gain in accuracy of statement or in force or clearness of expression, the author has freely changed, added to, or left out, what he originally wrote. To many of the Essays has been added a short note of the circumstances under which they were written. It is needless to say that any product of Mr. Freeman's pen is worthy of attentive perusal; and it is believed that the contents of this volume will throw light on several subjects of great historical importance and the widest interest. The following is a list of the subjects:*—I. "*The Mythical and Romantic Elements in Early English History;*" II. "*The Continuity of English History;*" III. "*The Relations between the Crowns of England and Scotland;*" IV. "*St. Thomas of Canterbury and his Biographers;*" V. "*The Reign of Edward the Third;*" VI. "*The Holy Roman Empire;*" VII. "*The Franks and the Gauls;*" VIII. "*The Early Sieges of Paris;*" IX. "*Frederick the First, King of Italy;*" X. "*The Emperor Frederick the Second;*" XI. "*Charles the Bold;*" XII. "*Presidential Government.*"—"*All of them are well worth reading, and very agreeable to read. He never touches a question without adding to our comprehension of it, without leaving the impression of an ample knowledge, a righteous purpose, a clear and powerful understanding."*—SATURDAY REVIEW.

Garnett.—IDYLLS AND EPIGRAMS. Chiefly from the Greek Anthology. By RICHARD GARNETT. Fcap. 8vo. 2s. 6d.

"A charming little book. For English readers, Mr. Garnett's translations will open a new world of thought."—WESTMINSTER REVIEW.

Geikie.—SCENERY OF SCOTLAND, viewed in Connexion with its Physical Geology. By ARCHIBALD GEIKIE, F.R.S., Director of the Geological Survey of Scotland. With Illustrations and a New Geological Map. Crown 8vo. 10s. 6d.

"Before long, we doubt not, it will be one of the travelling companions of every cultivated tourist in Scotland."—EDINBURGH COURANT. *"Amusing, picturesque, and instructive."*—TIMES. *"There is probably no one who has so thoroughly mastered the geology of Scotland as Mr. Geikie."*—PALL MALL GAZETTE.

Gladstone.—JUVENTUS MUNDI. The Gods and Men of the Heroic Age. By the Right Hon. W. E. GLADSTONE, M.P. Crown 8vo. cloth extra. With Map. 10s. 6d. Second Edition.

"This new work of Mr. Gladstone deals especially with the historic element in Homer, expounding that element and furnishing by its aid a full account of the Homeric men and the Homeric religion. It starts, after the introductory chapter, with a discussion of the several races then existing in Hellas, including the influence of the Phœnicians and Egyptians. It contains chapters "On the Olympian System, with its several Deities;" "On the Ethics and the Polity of the Heroic Age;" "On the Geography of Homer;" "On the Characters of the Poems;" presenting, in fine, a view of primitive life and primitive society as found in the poems of Homer. To this New Edition various additions have been made. "To read these brilliant details," says the ATHENÆUM, "is like standing on the Olympian threshold and gazing at the ineffable brightness within." According to the WESTMINSTER REVIEW, "it would be difficult to point out a book that contains so much fulness of knowledge along with so much freshness of perception and clearness of presentation."

Globe Library.—See end of this CATALOGUE.

Golden Treasury of the best Songs and Lyrical
POEMS IN THE ENGLISH LANGUAGE.—See GOLDEN
TREASURY SERIES.

Golden Treasury Series.—See end of this CATALOGUE.

Goldsmith's Works.—See GLOBE LIBRARY.

Guesses at Truth.—By TWO BROTHERS. With Vignette
Title, and Frontispiece. New Edition, with Memoir. Fcap. 8vo. 6s.
Also see Golden Treasury Series.

> These "*Guesses at Truth*" *are not intended to tell the reader what to think. They are rather meant to serve the purpose of a quarry in which, if one is building up his opinions for himself, and only wants to be provided with materials, he may meet with many things to suit him. To very many, since its publication, has this book proved a stimulus to earnest thought and noble action; and thus, to no small extent, it is believed, has it influenced the general current of thinking during the last forty years. It is now no secret that the authors were* AUGUSTUS *and* JULIUS CHARLES HARE. *"They—living as they did in constant and free interchange of thought on questions of philosophy and literature and art; delighting, each of them, in the epigrammatic terseness which is the charm of the 'Pensées' of Pascal, and the 'Caractères' of La Bruyère—agreed to utter themselves in this form, and the book appeared, anonymously, in two volumes, in* 1827."

Hamerton.—Works by PHILIP GILBERT HAMERTON :—

A PAINTER'S CAMP. Second Edition, revised. Extra fcap.
8vo. 6s.
BOOK I. *In England;* BOOK II. *In Scotland;* BOOK III. *In France.*

> *This is the story of an Artist's encampments and adventures. The headings of a few chapters may serve to convey a notion of the character of the book: A Walk on the Lancashire Moors; the Author his own Housekeeper and Cook; Tents and Boats for the*

Hamerton—*continued.*

Highlands; The Author encamps on an uninhabited Island; A Lake Voyage; A Gipsy Journey to Glencoe; Concerning Moonlight and Old Castles; A little French City; A Farm in the Autunois, &c. &c. "*These pages, written with infinite spirit and humour, bring into close rooms, back upon tired heads, the breezy airs of Lancashire moors and Highland lochs, with a freshness which no recent novelist has succeeded in preserving.*"—NONCONFORMIST. "*His pages sparkle with many turns of expression, not a few well-told anecdotes, and many observations which are the fruit of attentive study and wise reflection on the complicated phenomena of human life, as well as of unconscious nature.*"—WESTMINSTER REVIEW.

ETCHING AND ETCHERS. A Treatise Critical and Practical. With Original Plates by REMBRANDT, CALLOT, DUJARDIN, PAUL POTTER, &c. Royal 8vo. Half morocco. 31s. 6d.

"*The work is one which deserves to be consulted by every intelligent admirer of the fine arts, whether he is an etcher or not.*"—GUARDIAN.

"*It is not often we get anything like the combined intellectual and æsthetic treat which is supplied us by Mr. Hamerton's ably written and handsome volume. It is a work of which author, printer, and publisher may alike feel proud. It is a work, too, of which none but a genuine artist could by possibility have been the author.*"—SATURDAY REVIEW.

Hervey.—Works by ROSAMOND HERVEY :—

THE AARBERGS. Two vols. Crown 8vo. cloth. 21s.

"*All who can relish the more delicate flavour of thoughtfulness and sentiment enriching the quiet tone of common life will accept with gratitude a story so refined and wholesome.*"—GUARDIAN. "*A singularly pleasant book.*"—DAILY NEWS.

DUKE ERNEST, a Tragedy; and other Poems. Fcap. 8vo. 6s.

"*Conceived in pure taste and true historic feeling, and presented with much dramatic force. . . . . Thoroughly original.*"—BRITISH QUARTERLY.

Higginson.—MALBONE: An Oldport Romance. By T. W. HIGGINSON. Fcap. 8vo. 2s. 6d.

> This is a story of American life, so told as to be interesting and instructive to all English readers. The DAILY NEWS says: "Who likes a quiet story, full of mature thought, of clear humorous surprises, of artistic studious design? 'Malbone' is a rare work, possessing these characteristics, and replete, too, with honest literary effort."

Home.—BLANCHE LISLE, and other Poems. By CECIL HOME. Fcap. 8vo. 4s. 6d.

Hood (Tom).—THE PLEASANT TALE OF PUSS AND ROBIN AND THEIR FRIENDS, KITTY AND BOB. Told in Pictures by L. FRÖLICH, and in Rhymes by TOM HOOD. Crown 8vo. gilt. 3s. 6d.

> This is a pleasant little tale of wee Bob and his Sister, and their attempts to rescue poor Robin from the cruel claws of Pussy. It will be intelligible and interesting to the meanest capacity, and is illustrated by thirteen graphic cuts drawn by Frölich. "The volume is prettily got up, and is sure to be a favourite in the nursery." —SCOTSMAN. "Herr Frölich has outdone himself in his pictures of this dramatic chase."—MORNING POST.

Jebb.—THE CHARACTERS OF THEOPHRASTUS. An English Translation from a Revised Text. With Introduction and Notes. By R. C. JEBB, M.A., Fellow and Assistant Tutor of Trinity College, Cambridge, and Public Orator of the University. Extra fcap. 8vo. 6s. 6d.

> The first object of this book is to make these lively pictures of old Greek manners better known to English readers. But as the Editor and Translator has been at considerable pains to procure a reliable text, and has recorded the results of his critical labours in a lengthy Introduction, in Notes and Appendices, it is hoped that the work will prove of value even to the scholar. "We must not omit to give due honour to Mr. Jebb's translation, which is as good as translation can be. . . . Not less commendable are the execution of the Notes and the critical handling of the text."—SPECTATOR. "Mr. Jebb's little volume is more easily taken up than laid down."—GUARDIAN.

Jest Book.—By MARK LEMON.—See GOLDEN TREASURY SERIES.

Keary (A.)—Works by Miss A. KEARY:—

JANET'S HOME. Cheap Edition. Globe 8vo. 2s. 6d.

"*Never did a more charming family appear upon the canvas; and most skilfully and felicitously have their characters been portrayed. Each individual of the fireside is a finished portrait, distinct and lifelike. . . . The future before her as a novelist is that of becoming the Miss Austin of her generation.*"—SUN.

CLEMENCY FRANKLYN. Globe 8vo. 2s. 6d.

"*Full of wisdom and goodness, simple, truthful, and artistic. . . It is capital as a story; better still in its pure tone and wholesome influence.*"—GLOBE.

OLDBURY. Three vols. Crown 8vo. 31s. 6d.

"*This is a very powerfully written story.*"—GLOBE. "*This is a really excellent novel.*"—ILLUSTRATED LONDON NEWS. "*The sketches of society in Oldbury are excellent. The pictures of child life are full of truth.*"—WESTMINSTER REVIEW.

Keary (A. and E.)—Works by A. and E. KEARY:—

THE LITTLE WANDERLIN, and other Fairy Tales. 18mo. 3s. 6d.

"*The tales are fanciful and well written, and they are sure to win favour amongst little readers.*"—ATHENÆUM.

THE HEROES OF ASGARD. Tales from Scandinavian Mythology. New and Revised Edition, illustrated by HUARD. Extra fcap. 8vo. 4s. 6d.

"*Told in a light and amusing style, which, in its drollery and quaintness, reminds us of our old favourite Grimm.*"—TIMES.

Kingsley.—Works by the Rev. CHARLES KINGSLEY, M.A., Rector of Eversley, and Canon of Chester:—

Mr. Canon Kingsley's novels, most will admit, have not only commanded for themselves a foremost place in literature, as artistic

Kingsley (C.)—*continued*.

productions of a high class, but have exercised upon the age an incalculable influence in the direction of the highest Christian manliness. Mr. Kingsley has done more perhaps than almost any other writer of fiction to fashion the generation into whose hands the destinies of the world are now being committed. His works will therefore be read by all who wish to have their hearts cheered and their souls stirred to noble endeavour; they must be read by all who wish to know the influences which moulded the men of this century.

"WESTWARD HO!" or, The Voyages and Adventures of Sir Amyas Leigh. Sixth Edition. Crown 8vo. 6s.

No other work conveys a more vivid idea of the surging, adventurous, nobly inquisitive spirit of the generations which immediately followed the Reformation in England. The daring deeds of the Elizabethan heroes are told with a freshness, an enthusiasm, and a truthfulness that can belong only to one who wishes he had been their leader. His descriptions of the luxuriant scenery of the then new-found Western land are acknowledged to be unmatched. FRASER'S MAGAZINE *calls it "almost the best historical novel of the day."*

TWO YEARS AGO. Fourth Edition. Crown 8vo. 6s.

"*Mr. Kingsley has provided us all along with such pleasant diversions—such rich and brightly tinted glimpses of natural history, such suggestive remarks on mankind, society, and all sorts of topics, that amidst the pleasure of the way, the circuit to be made will be by most forgotten.*"—GUARDIAN.

HYPATIA; or, New Foes with an Old Face. Fifth Edition. Crown 8vo. 6s.

The work is from beginning to end a series of fascinating pictures of strange phases of that strange primitive society; and no finer portrait has yet been given of the noble-minded lady who was faithful to martyrdom in her attachment to the classical creeds. No work affords a clearer notion of the many interesting problems which agitated the minds of men in those days, and which, in various phases, are again coming up for discussion at the present time.

Kingsley (C.)—*continued*.

HEREWARD THE WAKE—LAST OF THE ENGLISH. Crown 8vo. 6s.

> *Mr. Kingsley here tells the story of the final conflict of the two races, Saxons and Normans, as if he himself had borne a part in it. While as a work of fiction "Hereward" cannot fail to delight all readers, no better supplement to the dry history of the time could be put into the hands of the young, containing as it does so vivid a picture of the social and political life of the period.*

YEAST: A Problem. Fifth Edition. Crown 8vo. 5s.

> *In this production the author shows, in an interesting dramatic form, the state of fermentation in which the minds of many earnest men are with regard to some of the most important religious and social problems of the day.*

ALTON LOCKE. New Edition. With a New Preface. Crown 8vo. 4s. 6d.

> *This novel, which shows forth the evils arising from modern "caste," has done much to remove the unnatural barriers which existed between the various classes of society, and to establish a sympathy to some extent between the higher and lower grades of the social scale. Though written with a purpose, it is full of character and interest; the author shows, to quote the* SPECTATOR, *"what it is that constitutes the true Christian, God-fearing, man-living gentleman."*

AT LAST: A CHRISTMAS IN THE WEST INDIES. With numerous Illustrations. Second and Cheaper Edition. Crown 8vo. 10s. 6d.

> *Mr. Kingsley's dream of forty years was at last fulfilled, when he started on a Christmas expedition to the West Indies, for the purpose of becoming personally acquainted with the scenes which he has so vividly described in "Westward ho!" "In this book Mr. Kingsley revels in the gorgeous wealth of West Indian vegetation, bringing before us one marvel after another, alternately sating and piquing our curiosity. Whether we climb the cliffs with him, or peer over into narrow bays which are being hollowed out by the trade-surf, or wander through impenetrable forests, where the tops of the trees form a green cloud overhead, or gaze down glens which*

Kingsley (C.)—*continued.*

are watered by the clearest brooks, running through masses of palm and banana and all the rich variety of foliage, we are equally delighted and amazed."—ATHENÆUM.

THE WATER BABIES. A Fairy Tale for a Land Baby. New Edition, with additional Illustrations by Sir NOEL PATON, R.S.A., and P. SKELTON. Crown 8vo. cloth extra gilt. 5s.

"In fun, in humour, and in innocent imagination, as a child's book we do not know its equal."—LONDON REVIEW. *"Mr. Kingsley must have the credit of revealing to us a new order of life. . . . There is in the 'Water Babies' an abundance of wit, fun, good humour, geniality,* élan, go.*"*—TIMES.

THE HEROES; or, Greek Fairy Tales for my Children. With Coloured Illustrations. New Edition. 18mo. 4s. 6d.

"We do not think these heroic stories have ever been more attractively told. . . . There is a deep under-current of religious feeling traceable throughout its pages which is sure to influence young readers powerfully."—LONDON REVIEW. *"One of the children's books that will surely become a classic."*—NONCONFORMIST.

PHAETHON; or, Loose Thoughts for Loose Thinkers. Third Edition. Crown 8vo. 2s.

"The dialogue of 'Phaethon' has striking beauties, and its suggestions may meet half-way many a latent doubt, and, like a light breeze, lift from the soul clouds that are gathering heavily, and threatening to settle down in misty gloom on the summer of many a fair and promising young life."—SPECTATOR.

POEMS; including The Saint's Tragedy, Andromeda, Songs, Ballads, etc. Complete Collected Edition. Extra fcap. 8vo. 6s.

Canon Kingsley's poetical works have gained for their author, independently of his other works, a high and enduring place in literature, and are much sought after. The publishers have here collected the whole of them in a moderately-priced and handy volume. The SPECTATOR *calls "Andromeda" "the finest piece of English hexameter verse that has ever been written. It is a volume which many readers will be glad to possess."*

Kingsley (H.)—Works by HENRY KINGSLEY :—

TALES OF OLD TRAVEL. Re-narrated. With Eight full-page Illustrations by HUARD. Fourth Edition. Crown 8vo. cloth, extra gilt. 5s.

> *In this volume Mr. Henry Kingsley re-narrates, at the same time preserving much of the quaintness of the original, some of the most fascinating tales of travel contained in the collections of Hakluyt and others. The* CONTENTS *are:—Marco Polo; The Shipwreck of Pelsart; The Wonderful Adventures of Andrew Battel; The Wanderings of a Capuchin; Peter Carder; The Preservation of the* "*Terra Nova;*" *Spitzbergen; D'Ermenonville's Acclimatization Adventure; The Old Slave Trade; Miles Philips; The Sufferings of Robert Everard; John Fox; Alvaro Nunez; The Foundation of an Empire.* "*We know no better book for those who want knowledge or seek to refresh it. As for the* '*sensational,' most novels are tame compared with these narratives.*"—ATHENÆUM. "*Exactly the book to interest and to do good to intelligent and high-spirited boys.*"—LITERARY CHURCHMAN.

THE LOST CHILD. With Eight Illustrations by FRÖLICH. Crown 4to. cloth gilt. 3s. 6d.

> *This is an interesting story of a little boy, the son of an Australian shepherd and his wife, who lost himself in the bush, and who was, after much searching, found dead far up a mountain-side. It contains many illustrations from the well-known pencil of Frölich.* "*A pathetic story, and told so as to give children an interest in Australian ways and scenery.*"— GLOBE. "*Very charmingly and very touchingly told.*"—SATURDAY REVIEW.

Knatchbull-Hugessen.—Works by E. H. KNATCHBULL-HUGESSEN, M.P. :—

> *Mr. Knatchbull-Hugessen has won for himself a reputation as an inimitable teller of fairy-tales.* "*His powers,*" *says the* TIMES, "*are of a very high order; light and brilliant narrative flows from his pen, and is fed by an invention as graceful as it is inexhaustible.*" "*Children reading his stories,*" *the* SCOTSMAN *says,* "*or hearing them read, will have their minds refreshed and invigorated as much as their bodies would be by abundance of fresh air and exercise.*"

Knatchbull-Hugessen—*continued.*

> STORIES FOR MY CHILDREN. With Illustrations. Third Edition. Extra fcap. 8vo. 5s.
>
> *"The stories are charming, and full of life and fun."*—STANDARD. *"The author has an imagination as fanciful as Grimm himself, while some of his stories are superior to anything that Hans Christian Andersen has written."*—NONCONFORMIST.
>
> CRACKERS FOR CHRISTMAS. More Stories. With Illustrations by JELLICOE and ELWES. Fourth Edition. Crown 8vo. 5s.
>
> *"A fascinating little volume, which will make him friends in every household in which there are children."*—DAILY NEWS.
>
> MOONSHINE: Fairy Tales. With Illustrations by W. BRUNTON. Fourth Edition. Crown 8vo. cloth gilt. 5s.
>
> *Here will be found "an Ogre, a Dwarf, a Wizard, quantities of Elves and Fairies, and several animals who speak like mortal men and women." There are twelve stories and nine irresistible illustrations. "A volume of fairy tales, written not only for ungrown children, but for bigger, and if you are nearly worn out, or sick, or sorry, you will find it good reading."*—GRAPHIC. *"The most charming volume of fairy tales which we have ever read. . . . We cannot quit this very pleasant book without a word of praise to its illustrator. Mr. Brunton from first to last has done admirably."*—TIMES.

La Lyre Française.—See GOLDEN TREASURY SERIES.

Latham.—SERTUM SHAKSPERIANUM, Subnexis aliquot aliunde excerptis floribus. Latine reddidit Rev. H. LATHAM, M.A. Extra fcap. 8vo. 5s.

> Besides versions of Shakespeare, this volume contains, among other pieces, Gray's "Elegy," Campbell's "Hohenlinden," Wolfe's "Burial of Sir John Moore," and selections from Cowper and George Herbert.

Lemon.—THE LEGENDS OF NUMBER NIP. By MARK LEMON. With Illustrations by C. KEENE. New Edition. Extra fcap. 8vo. 2s. 6d.

Life and Times of Conrad the Squirrel. A Story for Children. By the Author of "Wandering Willie," "Effie's Friends," &c. With a Frontispiece by R. FARREN. Crown 8vo. 3s. 6d.

It is sufficient to commend this story of a Squirrel to the attention of readers, that it is by the author of the beautiful stories of "Wandering Willie" and "Effie's Friends." It is well calculated to make children take an intelligent and tender interest in the lower animals.

Little Estella, and other Fairy Tales for the Young. Royal 16mo. 3s. 6d.

"*This is a fine story, and we thank heaven for not being too wise to enjoy it.*"—DAILY NEWS.

Little Lucy's Wonderful Globe.—See YONGE, C. M.

Lowell.—AMONG MY BOOKS. Six Essays. Dryden—Witchcraft—Shakespeare once More—New England Two Centuries Ago—Lessing—Rousseau and the Sentimentalists. Crown 8vo. 7s. 6d.

"*We may safely say the volume is one of which our chief complaint must be that there is not more of it. There are good sense and lively feeling forcibly and tersely expressed in every page of his writing.*"—PALL MALL GAZETTE.

Lyttelton.—Works by LORD LYTTELTON :—

THE "COMUS" OF MILTON, rendered into Greek Verse. Extra fcap. 8vo. 5s.

THE "SAMSON AGONISTES" OF MILTON, rendered into Verse. Extra fcap. 8vo. 6s. 6d.

"*Classical in spirit, full of force, and true to the original.*"—GUARDIAN.

Macmillan's Magazine.—Published Monthly. Price 1s. Volumes I. to XXV. are now ready. 7s. 6d. each.

Macquoid.—PATTY. By KATHERINE S. MACQUOID. Two vols. Crown 8vo. 21s.

The ATHENÆUM *"congratulates Mrs. Macquoid on having made a great step since the publication of her last novel," and says this " is a graceful and eminently readable story."* The GLOBE *considers it "well-written, amusing, and interesting, and has the merit of being out of the ordinary run of novels."*

Malbone.—See HIGGINSON.

Marlitt (E.)—THE COUNTESS GISELA. Translated from the German of E. MARLITT. Crown 8vo. 7s. 6d.

"*A very beautiful story of German country life.*"—LITERARY CHURCHMAN.

Masson (Professor).—Works by DAVID MASSON, M.A., Professor of Rhetoric and English Literature in the University of Edinburgh. (See also BIOGRAPHICAL and PHILOSOPHICAL CATALOGUES.)

ESSAYS, BIOGRAPHICAL AND CRITICAL. Chiefly on the British Poets. 8vo. 12s. 6d.

"*Distinguished by a remarkable power of analysis, a clear statement of the actual facts on which speculation is based, and an appropriate beauty of language. These Essays should be popular with serious men.*"—ATHENÆUM.

BRITISH NOVELISTS AND THEIR STYLES. Being a Critical Sketch of the History of British Prose Fiction. Crown 8vo. 7s. 6d.

"*Valuable for its lucid analysis of fundamental principles, its breadth of view, and sustained animation of style.*"—SPECTATOR. "*Mr. Masson sets before us with a bewitching ease and clearness which nothing but a perfect mastery of his subject could have rendered possible, a large body of both deep and sound discriminative criticism on all the most memorable of our British novelists. . . . . His brilliant and instructive book.*"—JOHN BULL.

Merivale.—KEATS' HYPERION, rendered into Latin Verse. By C. MERIVALE, B.D. Second Edition. Extra fcap. 8vo. 3s. 6d.

Milner.—THE LILY OF LUMLEY. By EDITH MILNER. Crown 8vo. 7s. 6d.

"*The novel is a good one and decidedly worth the reading.*"— EXAMINER. "*A pretty, brightly-written story.*" — LITERARY CHURCHMAN. "*A tale possessing the deepest interest.*"—COURT JOURNAL.

Mistral (F.)—MIRELLE, a Pastoral Epic of Provence. Translated by H. CRICHTON. Extra fcap. 8vo. 6s.

"*It would be hard to overpraise the sweetness and pleasing freshness of this charming epic.*"—ATHENÆUM. "*A good translation of a poem that deserves to be known by all students of literature and friends of old-world simplicity in story-telling.*" — NONCONFORMIST.

Brown, M.P.—MR. PISISTRATUS BROWN, M.P., IN THE HIGHLANDS. Reprinted from the *Daily News*, with Additions. Crown 8vo. 5s.

These papers appeared at intervals in the DAILY NEWS *during the summer of* 1871. *They narrate in light and jocular style the adventures "by flood and field" of Mr. Brown, M.P. and his friend in their tour through the West Highlands, and will be found well adapted to while away a pleasant hour either by the winter fireside or during a summer holiday.*

Mrs. Jerningham's Journal. A Poem purporting to be the Journal of a newly-married Lady. Second Edition. Fcap. 8vo. 3s. 6d.

"*It is nearly a perfect gem. We have had nothing so good for a long time, and those who neglect to read it are neglecting one of the jewels of contemporary history.*"—EDINBURGH DAILY REVIEW. "*One quality in the piece, sufficient of itself to claim a moment's attention, is that it is unique—original, indeed, is not too strong a word—in the manner of its conception and execution.*" —PALL MALL GAZETTE.

Mitford (A. B.)—TALES OF OLD JAPAN. By A. B. MITFORD, Second Secretary to the British Legation in Japan. With Illustrations drawn and cut on Wood by Japanese Artists. Two Vols. Crown 8vo. 21s.

The old Japanese civilization is fast disappearing, and will, in a few years, be completely extinct. It was important, therefore, to preserve as far as possible trustworthy records of a state of society which, although venerable from its antiquity, has for Europeans the charm of novelty; hence the series of narratives and legends translated by Mr. Mitford, and in which the Japanese are very judiciously left to tell their own tale. The two volumes comprise not only stories and episodes illustrative of Asiatic superstitions, but also three sermons. The Preface, Appendices, and Notes explain a number of local peculiarities; the thirty-one woodcuts are the genuine work of a native artist, who, unconsciously of course, has adopted the process first introduced by the early German masters. "They will always be interesting as memorials of a most exceptional society; while, regarded simply as tales, they are sparkling, sensational, and dramatic, and the originality of their ideas and the quaintness of their language give them a most captivating piquancy. The illustrations are extremely interesting, and for the curious in such matters have a special and particular value."—PALL MALL GAZETTE.

Morte d'Arthur.—See GLOBE LIBRARY.

Myers (Ernest).—THE PURITANS. By ERNEST MYERS. Extra fcap. 8vo. cloth. 2s. 6d.

"*It is not too much to call it a really grand poem, stately and dignified, and showing not only a high poetic mind, but also great power over poetic expression.*"—LITERARY CHURCHMAN.

Myers (F. W. H.)—POEMS. By F. W. H. MYERS. Containing "St. Paul," "St. John," and others. Extra fcap. 8vo. 4s. 6d.

"*It is rare to find a writer who combines to such an extent the faculty of communicating feelings with the faculty of euphonious expression.*"—SPECTATOR. "'*St. Paul*' *stands without a rival as the noblest religious poem which has been written in an age which beyond any other has been prolific in this class of poetry. The sublimest conceptions are expressed in language which, for richness, taste, and purity, we have never seen excelled.*"—JOHN BULL.

Nine Years Old.—By the Author of "St. Olave's," "When I was a Little Girl," &c. Illustrated by FRÖLICH. Second Edition. Extra fcap. 8vo. cloth gilt. 4s. 6d.

It is believed that this story, by the favourably known author of "St. Olave's," will be found both highly interesting and instructive to the young. The volume contains eight graphic illustrations by Mr. L. Frölich. The EXAMINER says: "Whether the readers are nine years old, or twice, or seven times as old, they must enjoy this pretty volume."

Noel.—BEATRICE, AND OTHER POEMS. By the Hon. RODEN NOEL. Fcap. 8vo. 6s.

"It is impossible to read the poem through without being powerfully moved. There are passages in it which for intensity and tenderness, clear and vivid vision, spontaneous and delicate sympathy, may be compared with the best efforts of our best living writers."—SPECTATOR. "It is long since we have seen a volume of poems which has seemed to us so full of the real stuff of which we are made, and uttering so freely the deepest wants of this complicate age."—BRITISH QUARTERLY.

Norton.—Works by the Hon. Mrs. NORTON :—

THE LADY OF LA GARAYE. With Vignette and Frontispiece. New Edition. Fcap. 8vo. 4s. 6d.

"A poem entirely unaffected, perfectly original, so true and yet so fanciful, so strong and yet so womanly, with painting so exquisite, a pure portraiture of the highest affections and the deepest sorrows, and instilling a lesson true, simple, and sublime."— DUBLIN UNIVERSITY MAGAZINE. "Full of thought well expressed, and may be classed among her best efforts."—TIMES.

OLD SIR DOUGLAS. Cheap Edition. Globe 8vo. 2s. 6d.

"This varied and lively novel—this clever novel so full of character and of fine incidental remark."—SCOTSMAN. "One of the pleasantest and healthiest stories of modern fiction."—GLOBE.

Oliphant.—Works by Mrs. OLIPHANT :—

AGNES HOPETOUN'S SCHOOLS AND HOLIDAYS. New Edition with Illustrations. Royal 16mo. gilt leaves. 4s. 6d.

"There are few books of late years more fitted to touch the heart, purify the feeling, and quicken and sustain right principles."— NONCONFORMIST. "A more gracefully written story it is impossible to desire."—DAILY NEWS.

Oliphant—*continued.*

A SON OF THE SOIL. New Edition. Globe 8vo. 2s. 6d.

"*It is a very different work from the ordinary run of novels. The whole life of a man is portrayed in it, worked out with subtlety and insight.*"—ATHENÆUM. "*With entire freedom from any sensational plot, there is enough of incident to give keen interest to the narrative, and make us feel as we read it that we have been spending a few hours with friends who will make our own lives better by their own noble purposes and holy living.*"—BRITISH QUARTERLY REVIEW.

Our Year. A Child's Book, in Prose and Verse. By the Author of "John Halifax, Gentleman." Illustrated by CLARENCE DOBELL. Royal 16mo. 3s. 6d.

"*It is just the book we could wish to see in the hands of every child.*" —ENGLISH CHURCHMAN.

Olrig Grange. Edited by HERMANN KUNST, Philol. Professor. Extra fcap. 8vo. 6s. 6d.

This is a poem in six parts, each the utterance of a distinct person. It is the story of a young Scotchman of noble aims designed for the ministry, but who "rent the Creed trying to fit it on," who goes to London to seek fame and fortune in literature, and who returns dejected to his old home in the north to die. The NORTH BRITISH DAILY MAIL, *in reviewing the work, speaks of it as affording "abounding evidence of genial and generative faculty working in self-decreed modes. A masterly and original power of impression, pouring itself forth in clear, sweet, strong rhythm. . . . Easy to cull, remarkable instances of thrilling fervour, of glowing delicacy, of scathing and trenchant scorn, to point out the fine and firm discrimination of character which prevails throughout, to dwell upon the ethical power and psychological truth which are exhibited, to note the skill with which the diverse parts of the poem are set in organic relation. . . . It is a fine poem, full of life, of music, and of clear vision.*"

Oxford Spectator, the.—Reprinted. Extra fcap. 8vo. 3s. 6d.

These papers, after the manner of Addison's "Spectator," appeared in Oxford from November 1867 *to December* 1868, *at intervals* varying from two days to a week. They attempt to sketch several features of Oxford life from an undergraduate's point of view, and to give modern readings of books which undergraduates study. "There is," the SATURDAY REVIEW says, "all the old fun, the old sense of social ease and brightness and freedom, the old medley of work and indolence, of jest and earnest, that made Oxford life so picturesque."

Palgrave.—Works by FRANCIS TURNER PALGRAVE, M.A., late Fellow of Exeter College, Oxford :—

ESSAYS ON ART. Extra fcap. 8vo. 6s.

Mulready—Dyce—Holman Hunt—Herbert—Poetry, Prose, and Sensationalism in Art—Sculpture in England—The Albert Cross, &c. Most of these Essays have appeared in the SATURDAY REVIEW *and elsewhere; but they have been minutely revised, and in some cases almost re-written, with the aim mainly of excluding matters of temporary interest, and softening down all asperities of censure. The main object of the book is, by examples taken chiefly from the works of contemporaries, to illustrate the truths, that art has fixed principles, of which any one may attain the knowledge who is not wanting in natural taste. Art, like poetry, is addressed to the world at large, not to a special jury of professional masters. " In many respects the truest critic we have."*—LITERARY CHURCHMAN.

THE FIVE DAYS' ENTERTAINMENTS AT WENTWORTH GRANGE. A Book for Children. With Illustrations by ARTHUR HUGHES and Engraved Title-page by JEENS. Small 4to. cloth extra. 6s.

"*If you want a really good book for both sexes and all ages, buy this, as handsome a volume of tales as you'll find in all the market.*"—ATHENÆUM. "*Exquisite both in form and substance.*" —GUARDIAN.

LYRICAL POEMS. Extra fcap. 8vo. 6s.

"*A volume of pure quiet verse, sparkling with tender melodies, and alive with thoughts of genuine poetry. . . . Turn where we will throughout the volume, we find traces of beauty, tenderness, and truth; true poet's work, touched and refined by the master-hand of a real artist, who shows his genius even in trifles.*"—STANDARD.

Palgrave—*continued.*

ORIGINAL HYMNS. Third Edition, enlarged, 18mo. 1s. 6d.

"*So choice, so perfect, and so refined, so tender in feeling, and so scholarly in expression, that we look with special interest to everything that he gives us.*"—LITERARY CHURCHMAN.

GOLDEN TREASURY OF THE BEST SONGS AND LYRICS. Edited by F. T. PALGRAVE. See GOLDEN TREASURY SERIES.

SHAKESPEARE'S SONNETS AND SONGS. Edited by F. T. PALGRAVE. Gem Edition. With Vignette Title by JEENS. 3s. 6d.

"*For minute elegance no volume could possibly excel the 'Gem Edition.'*"—SCOTSMAN.

Palmer's Book of Praise.—See GOLDEN TREASURY SERIES.

Parables.—TWELVE PARABLES OF OUR LORD. Illustrated in Colours from Sketches taken in the East by McENIRY, with Frontispiece from a Picture by JOHN JELLICOE, and Illuminated Texts and Borders. Royal 4to. in Ornamental Binding. 16s.

The SCOTSMAN *calls this "one of the most superb books of the season." The richly and tastefully illuminated borders are from the* Brevario Grimani, *in St. Mark's Library, Venice. The* TIMES *calls it "one of the most beautiful of modern pictorial works;" while the* GRAPHIC *says "nothing in this style, so good, has ever before been published."*

Patmore.—THE ANGEL IN THE HOUSE. By COVENTRY PATMORE.

BOOK I. *The Betrothal;* BOOK II. *The Espousals;* BOOK III. *Faithful for Ever. The Victories of Love. Tamerton Church Tower.* Two Vols. Fcap. 8vo. 12s.

"*A style combining much of the homeliness of Crabbe, with sweeter music and a far higher range of thought.*"—TIMES. "*Its merit is more than sufficient to account for its success. . . . In its manly and healthy cheer, the 'Angel in the House' is an effectual protest against the morbid poetry of the age.*"—EDINBURGH REVIEW.

"*We think his 'Angel in the House' would be a good wedding-gift to a bridegroom from his friends; though, whenever it is read with a right view of its aim, we believe it will be found itself, more or less, of an angel in the house.*"—FRASER'S MAGAZINE.

*** *A New and Cheap Edition in One Vol. 18mo., beautifully printed on toned paper, price* 2s. 6d.

Pember.—THE TRAGEDY OF LESBOS. A Dramatic Poem. By E. H PEMBER. Fcap. 8vo. 4s. 6d.

Founded upon the story of Sappho. "He tells his story with dramatic force, and in language that often rises almost to grandeur."—ATHENÆUM.

Poole.—PICTURES OF COTTAGE LIFE IN THE WEST OF ENGLAND. By MARGARET E. POOLE. New and Cheaper Edition. With Frontispiece by R. Farren. Crown 8vo. 3s. 6d.

"*Charming stories of peasant life, written in something of George Eliot's style. . . . Her stories could not be other than they are, as literal as truth, as romantic as fiction, full of pathetic touches and strokes of genuine humour. . . . All the stories are studies of actual life, executed with no mean art.*"—TIMES.

Pope's Poetical Works.—See GLOBE LIBRARY.

Population of an Old Pear Tree. From the French of E. VAN BRUYSSEL. Edited by the Author of "The Heir of Redclyffe." With Illustrations by BECKER. Second Edition. Crown 8vo. gilt edges. 6s.

"*This is not a regular book of natural history, but a description of all the living creatures that came and went in a summer's day beneath an old pear tree, observed by eyes that had for the nonce become microscopic, recorded by a pen that finds dramas in everything, and illustrated by a dainty pencil. . . . We can hardly fancy anyone with a moderate turn for the curiosities of insect life, or for delicate French esprit, not being taken by these clever sketches.*"—GUARDIAN. "*A whimsical and charming little book.*" —ATHENÆUM.

Portfolio of Cabinet Pictures.—Oblong folio, price 42s.

This is a handsome portfolio containing faithfully executed and beautifully coloured reproductions of five well-known pictures:— "Childe Harold's Pilgrimage" and "The Fighting Téméraire," by J. M. W. Turner; "Crossing the Bridge," by Sir W. A. Callcott; "The Cornfield," by John Constable; and "A Landscape," by Birket Foster. The DAILY NEWS *says of them, "They are very beautifully executed, and might be framed and hung up on the wall, as creditable substitutes for the originals."*

Raphael of Urbino and his Father Giovanni SANTI.—By J. D. PASSAVANT, formerly Director of the Museum at Frankfort. Illustrated. Royal 8vo. cloth gilt, gilt edges. 31s. 6d.

To the enlarged French edition of Herr Passavant's Life of Raphael, that painter's admirers have turned whenever they have sought for information; and it will doubtless remain for many years the best book of reference on all questions pertaining to the great painter. The present work consists of a translation of those parts of Passavant's volumes which are most likely to interest the general reader. Besides a complete life of Raphael it contains the valuable descriptions of all his known paintings, and the Chronological Index, which is of so much service to amateurs who wish to study the progressive character of his works. The illustrations, twenty in number, by Woodbury's new permanent process of photography, are from the finest engravings that could be procured, and have been chosen with the intention of giving examples of Raphael's various styles of painting. "There will be found in the volume almost all that the ordinary student or critic would require to learn."— ART JOURNAL. *"It is most beautifully and profusely illustrated."—* SATURDAY REVIEW.

Realmah.—By the Author of "Friends in Council." Crown 8vo. 6s.

Rhoades.—POEMS. By JAMES RHOADES. Fcap. 8vo. 4s. 6d.
  CONTENTS:—*Ode to Harmony; To the Spirit of Unrest; Ode to Winter; The Tunnel; To the Spirit of Beauty; Song of a Leaf;*

By the Rother; An Old Orchard; Love and Rest; The Flowers Surprised; On the Death of Artemus Ward; The Two Paths; The Ballad of Little Maisie; Sonnets.

Richardson.—THE ILIAD OF THE EAST. A Selection of Legends drawn from Valmiki's Sanskrit Poem, "The Ramayana." By FREDERIKA RICHARDSON. Crown 8vo. 7s. 6d.

"*It is impossible to read it without recognizing the value and interest of the Eastern epic. It is as fascinating as a fairy tale, this romantic poem of India.*"—GLOBE. "*A charming volume which at once enmeshes the reader in its snares.*"—ATHENÆUM.

Robinson Crusoe.—See GLOBE LIBRARY and GOLDEN TREASURY SERIES.

Roby.—STORY OF A HOUSEHOLD, AND OTHER POEMS. By MARY K. ROBY. Fcap. 8vo. 5s.

Rogers.—Works by J. E. ROGERS:—

RIDICULA REDIVIVA. Old Nursery Rhymes. Illustrated in Colours, with Ornamental Cover. Crown 4to. 6s.

"*The most splendid, and at the same time the most really meritorious of the books specially intended for children, that we have seen.*"—SPECTATOR. "*These large bright pictures will attract children to really good and honest artistic work, and that ought not to be an indifferent consideration with parents who propose to educate their children.*"—PALL MALL GAZETTE.

MORES RIDICULI. Old Nursery Rhymes. Illustrated in Colours, with Ornamental Cover. Crown 4to. 6s.

"*These world-old rhymes have never had and need never wish for a better pictorial setting than Mr. Rogers has given them.*"—TIMES. "*Nothing could be quainter or more absurdly comical than most of the pictures, which are all carefully executed and beautifully coloured.*"—GLOBE.

Rossetti.—Works by CHRISTINA ROSSETTI:—

GOBLIN MARKET, AND OTHER POEMS. With two Designs by D. G. ROSSETTI. Second Edition. Fcap. 8vo. 5s.

Rossetti—*continued.*

"*She handles her little marvel with that rare poetic discrimination which neither exhausts it of its simple wonders by pushing symbolism too far, nor keeps those wonders in the merely fabulous and capricious stage. In fact, she has produced a true children's poem, which is far more delightful to the mature than to children, though it would be delightful to all.*"—SPECTATOR.

THE PRINCE'S PROGRESS, AND OTHER POEMS. With two Designs by D. G. ROSSETTI. Fcap. 8vo. 6s.

"*Miss Rossetti's poems are of the kind which recalls Shelley's definition of Poetry as the record of the best and happiest moments of the best and happiest minds. . . . They are like the piping of a bird on the spray in the sunshine, or the quaint singing with which a child amuses itself when it forgets that anybody is listening.*"—SATURDAY REVIEW.

Rossetti (W. M.)—DANTE'S HELL. See "DANTE."

Ruth and her Friends. A Story for Girls. With a Frontispiece. Fourth Edition. Royal 16mo. 3s. 6d.

"*We wish all the school girls and home-taught girls in the land had the opportunity of reading it.*"—NONCONFORMIST.

Scott's Poetical Works.—See GLOBE LIBRARY.

Scouring of the White Horse; or, the Long VACATION RAMBLE OF A LONDON CLERK. Illustrated by DOYLE. Imp. 16mo. Cheaper Issue. 3s. 6d.

"*A glorious tale of summer joy.*"—FREEMAN. "*There is a genial hearty life about the book.*"—JOHN BULL. "*The execution is excellent. . . . Like 'Tom Brown's School Days,' the 'White Horse' gives the reader a feeling of gratitude and personal esteem towards the author.*"—SATURDAY REVIEW.

Seeley (Professor).—LECTURES AND ESSAYS. By J. R. SEELEY, M.A. Professor of Modern History in the University of Cambridge. 8vo. 10s. 6d.

CONTENTS:—*Roman Imperialism:* 1. *The Great Roman Revolution;* 2. *The Proximate Cause of the Fall of the Roman Empire;* 3. *The Later Empire.*—*Milton's Political Opinions—Milton's Poetry—Elementary Principles in Art—Liberal Education in Universities—English in Schools—The Church as a Teacher of Morality—The Teaching of Politics: an Inaugural Lecture delivered at Cambridge.* "He is the master of a clear and pleasant style, great facility of expression, and a considerable range of illustration. . . . The criticism is always acute, the description always graphic and continuous, and the matter of each essay is carefully arranged with a view to unity of effect."—SPECTATOR. "His book will be full of interest to all thoughtful readers."—PALL MALL GAZETTE.

Shairp (Principal).—KILMAHOE, a Highland Pastoral, with other Poems. By JOHN CAMPBELL SHAIRP, Principal of the United College, St. Andrews. Fcap. 8vo. 5s.

"*Kilmahoe is a Highland Pastoral,* redolent *of the warm soft air of the western lochs and moors,* sketched *out with* remarkable *grace and picturesqueness.*"—SATURDAY REVIEW.

Shakespeare.—The Works of WILLIAM SHAKESPEARE. Cambridge Edition. Edited by W. GEORGE CLARK, M.A. and W. ALDIS WRIGHT, M.A. Nine vols. 8vo. Cloth. 4*l.* 14*s.* 6*d.*

This, now acknowledged to be the standard edition of Shakespeare, is the result of many years' study and research on the part of the accomplished Editors, assisted by the suggestions and contributions of Shakespearian students in all parts of the country. The following are the distinctive characteristics of this edition:—1. The text is based on a thorough collation of the four Folios, and of all the Quarto editions of the separate plays, and of subsequent editions and commentaries. 2. All the results of this collation are given in notes at the foot of the page, together with the conjectural emendations collected and suggested by the Editors, or furnished by their correspondents, so as to give the reader a complete view of the existing materials out of which the text has been constructed, or may be amended. 3. Where a quarto edition differs materially from the received text, the text of the quarto is printed literatim in a smaller type after the received text. 4. The lines in each scene are numbered separately, so as to facilitate reference. 5. At the end of each

*play a few notes, critical, explanatory, and illustrative, are added.
6. The Poems, edited on a similar plan, are printed at the end
of the Dramatic Works. The Preface contains some notes on
Shakespearian Grammar, Spelling, Metre, and Punctuation, and
a history of all the chief editions from the Poet's time to the present.
The* GUARDIAN *calls it an "excellent, and, to the student, almost
indispensable edition;" and the* EXAMINER *calls it "an unrivalled
edition."*

Shakespeare, Globe.—See GLOBE LIBRARY.

Shakespeare's Tempest. Edited with Glossarial and Explanatory Notes, by the Rev. J. M. JEPHSON. Second Edition. 18mo. 1s.

This is an edition for use in schools. The introduction treats briefly of the value of language, the fable of the play and other points. The notes are intended to teach the student to analyse every obscure sentence and trace out the logical sequence of the poet's thoughts; to point out the rules of Shakespeare's versification; to explain obsolete words and meanings; and to guide the student's taste by directing his attention to such passages as seem especially worthy of note for their poetical beauty or truth to nature. The text is in the main founded upon that of the first collected edition of Shakespeare's plays.

Smith.—POEMS. By CATHERINE BARNARD SMITH. Fcap. 8vo. 5s.

"*Wealthy in feeling, meaning, finish, and grace; not without passion, which is suppressed, but the keener for that.*"—ATHENÆUM.

Smith (Rev. Walter).—HYMNS OF CHRIST AND THE CHRISTIAN LIFE. By the Rev. WALTER C. SMITH, M.A. Fcap. 8vo. 6s.

"*These are among the sweetest sacred poems we have read for a long time. With no profuse imagery, expressing a range of feeling and expression by no means uncommon, they are true and elevated, and their pathos is profound and simple.*"—NONCONFORMIST.

Song Book, the.—See GOLDEN TREASURY SERIES.

Spenser's Works.—See GLOBE LIBRARY.

Spring Songs. By a WEST HIGHLANDER. With a Vignette Illustration by GOURLAY STEELE. Fcap. 8vo. 1s. 6d.

"*Without a trace of affectation or sentimentalism, these utterances are perfectly simple and natural, profoundly human and profoundly true.*"—DAILY NEWS.

Stephen (C. E.)—THE SERVICE OF THE POOR; being an Inquiry into the Reasons for and against the Establishment of Religious Sisterhoods for Charitable Purposes. By CAROLINE EMILIA STEPHEN. Crown 8vo. 6s. 6d.

Miss Stephen defines religious Sisterhoods as "associations, the organization of which is based upon the assumption that works of charity are either acts of worship in themselves, or means to an end, that end being the spiritual welfare of the objects or the performers of those works." Arguing from that point of view, she devotes the first part of her volume to a brief history of religious associations, taking as specimens—I. The Deaconesses of the Primitive Church; II. the Béguines; III. the Third Order of S. Francis; IV. the Sisters of Charity of S. Vincent de Paul; V. the Deaconesses of Modern Germany. In the second part, Miss Stephen attempts to show what are the real wants met by Sisterhoods, to what extent the same wants may be effectually met by the organization of corresponding institutions on a secular basis, and what are the reasons for endeavouring to do so. "It touches incidentally and with much wisdom and tenderness on so many of the relations of women, particularly of single women, with society, that it may be read with advantage by many who have never thought of entering a Sisterhood."—SPECTATOR.

Stephens (J. B.)—CONVICT ONCE. A Poem. By J. BRUNTON STEPHENS. Extra fcap. 8vo. 3s. 6d.

A tale of sin and sorrow, purporting to be the confession of Magdalen Power, a convict first, and then a teacher in one of the Australian Settlements; the narrative is supposed to be written by Hyacinth, a pupil of Magdalen Power, and the victim of her jealousy. The metre of the poem is the same as that of Longfellow's "Evangeline." "It is as far more interesting than ninety-nine novels out of a hundred, as it is superior to them in power, worth, and beauty. We should most strongly advise everybody to read 'Convict Once.'"—WESTMINSTER REVIEW.

Storehouse of Stories.—See YONGE, C. M.

Streets and Lanes of a City: Being the Reminiscences of AMY DUTTON. With a Preface by the BISHOP OF SALISBURY. Second and Cheaper Edition. Globe 8vo. 2s. 6d.

This little volume records, to use the words of the Bishop of Salisbury, "a portion of the experience, selected out of overflowing materials, of two ladies, during several years of devoted work as district parochial visitors in a large population in the north of England." Every incident narrated is absolutely true, and only the names of the persons introduced have been (necessarily) changed. The "Reminiscences of Amy Dutton" serve to illustrate the line of argument adopted by Miss Stephen in her work on "the Service of the Poor," because they show that as in one aspect the lady visitor may be said to be a link between rich and poor, in another she helps to blend the "religious" life with the "secular," and in both does service of extreme value to the Church and Nation. "One of the most really striking books that has ever come before us."—LITERARY CHURCHMAN.

Sunday Book of Poetry.—See GOLDEN TREASURY SERIES.

Symonds (J. A., M.D.)—MISCELLANIES. By JOHN ADDINGTON SYMONDS, M.D. Selected and Edited, with an Introductory Memoir, by his Son. 8vo. 7s. 6d.

The late Dr. Symonds, of Bristol, was a man of singularly versatile and elegant as well as powerful and scientific intellect. In order to make this selection from his many works generally interesting, the editor has confined himself to works of pure literature, and to such scientific studies as had a general philosophical or social interest. Among the general subjects are articles on the Principles of Beauty, on Knowledge, and a Life of Dr. Pritchard; among the Scientific Studies are papers on Sleep and Dreams, Apparitions, the Relations between Mind and Muscle, **Habit**, etc.; there are several papers on *the Social and Political Aspects of Medicine; and a few Poems and Translations, selected from a great number of equal merit, have been inserted at the end, as specimens of the lighter literary recreations which occupied the intervals of leisure in a long and laborious life. "Mr. Symonds has certainly done right in gathering together what his father left behind him."*—SATURDAY REVIEW.

Theophrastus, Characters of.—See JEBB.

Thring.—SCHOOL SONGS.   A Collection of Songs for Schools. With the Music arranged for four Voices.   Edited by the Rev. E. THRING and H. RICCIUS.   Folio.   7s. 6d.

There is a tendency in schools to stereotype the forms of life. Any genial solvent is valuable. Games do much; but games do not penetrate to domestic life, and are much limited by age. Music supplies the want. The collection includes the "Agnus Dei," Tennyson's "Light Brigade," Macaulay's "Ivry," etc. among other pieces.

Tom Brown's School Days.—By AN OLD BOY.
Golden Treasury Edition, 4s. 6d.   People's Edition, 2s.
With Sixty Illustrations, by A. HUGHES and SYDNEY HALL, Square, cloth extra, gilt edges.   10s. 6d.
With Seven Illustrations by the same Artists, Crown 8vo. 6s.

"We have read and re-read this book with unmingled pleasure. . . . We have carefully guarded ourselves against any tampering with our critical sagacity, and yet have been compelled again and again to exclaim, Bene! Optime!"—LONDON QUARTERLY REVIEW. *"An exact picture of the bright side of a Rugby boy's experience, told with a life, a spirit, and a fond minuteness of detail and recollection which is infinitely honourable to the author."*—EDINBURGH REVIEW.   *"The most famous boy's book in the language."*—DAILY NEWS.

Tom Brown at Oxford.—New Edition.   With Illustrations. Crown 8vo.   6s.

"In no other work that we can call to mind are the finer qualities of the English gentleman more happily portrayed."—DAILY NEWS. *"A book of great power and truth."*—NATIONAL REVIEW.

Trench.—Works by R. CHENEVIX TRENCH, D.D., Archbishop of Dublin. (For other Works by this Author, see THEOLOGICAL, HISTORICAL, and PHILOSOPHICAL CATALOGUES.)

POEMS. Collected and arranged anew. Fcap. 8vo. 7s. 6d.

ELEGIAC POEMS. Third Edition. Fcap. 8vo. 2s. 6d.

CALDERON'S LIFE'S A DREAM: The Great Theatre of the World. With an Essay on his Life and Genius. Fcap. 8vo. 4s. 6d.

HOUSEHOLD BOOK OF ENGLISH POETRY. Selected and arranged, with Notes, by Archbishop TRENCH. Second Edition. Extra fcap. 8vo. 5s. 6d.

This volume is called a "Household Book," by this name implying that it is a book for all—that there is nothing in it to prevent it from being confidently placed in the hands of every member of the household. Specimens of all classes of poetry are given, including selections from living authors. The editor has aimed to produce a book "which the emigrant, finding room for little not absolutely necessary, might yet find room for in his trunk, and the traveller in his knapsack, and that on some narrow shelves where there are few books this might be one." "The Archbishop has conferred in this delightful volume an important gift on the whole English-speaking population of the world."—PALL MALL GAZETTE.

SACRED LATIN POETRY, Chiefly Lyrical. Selected and arranged for Use. By Archbishop TRENCH. Second Edition, Corrected and Improved. Fcap. 8vo. 7s.

"The aim of the present volume is to offer to members of our English Church a collection of the best sacred Latin poetry, such as they shall be able entirely and heartily to accept and approve—a collection, that is, in which they shall not be evermore liable to be offended, and to have the current of their sympathies checked, by coming upon that which, however beautiful as poetry, out of higher respects they must reject and condemn—in which, too, they shall not fear that snares are being laid for them, to entangle them unawares in admiration for aught which is inconsistent with their faith and fealty to their own spiritual mother."—PREFACE.

JUSTIN MARTYR, AND OTHER POEMS. Fifth Edition. Fcap. 8vo. 6s.

Trollope (Anthony). — SIR HARRY HOTSPUR OF HUMBLETHWAITE. By ANTHONY TROLLOPE, Author of "Framley Parsonage," etc. Cheap Edition. Globe 8vo. 2s. 6d.

The TIMES says: "In this novel we are glad to recognize a return to what we must call Mr. Trollope's old form. The characters are drawn with vigour and boldness, and the book may do good to many readers of both sexes." The ATHENÆUM remarks: "No reader who begins to read this book is likely to lay it down until the last page is turned. This brilliant novel appears to us decidedly more successful than any other of Mr. Trollope's shorter stories."

Turner.—Works by the Rev. CHARLES TENNYSON TURNER :—

SONNETS. Dedicated to his Brother, the Poet Laureate. Fcap. 8vo. 4s. 6d.

"The Sonnets are dedicated to Mr. Tennyson by his brother, and have, independently of their merits, an interest of association. They both love to write in simple expressive Saxon; both love to touch their imagery in epithets rather than in formal similes; both have a delicate perception of rhythmical movement, and thus Mr. Turner has occasional lines which, for phrase and music, might be ascribed to his brother. . . He knows the haunts of the wild rose, the shady nooks where light quivers through the leaves, the ruralities, in short, of the land of imagination."—ATHENÆUM.

SMALL TABLEAUX. Fcap. 8vo. 4s. 6d.

"These brief poems have not only a peculiar kind of interest for the student of English poetry, but are intrinsically delightful, and will reward a careful and frequent perusal. Full of naïveté, piety, love, and knowledge of natural objects, and each expressing a single and generally a simple subject by means of minute and original pictorial touches, these Sonnets have a place of their own."—PALL MALL GAZETTE.

Virgil's Works.—See GLOBE LIBRARY.

Vittoria Colonna.—LIFE AND POEMS. By MRS. HENRY ROSCOE. Crown 8vo. 9s.

The life of Vittoria Colonna, the celebrated Marchesa di Pescara, has received but cursory notice from any English writer, though in every history of Italy her name is mentioned with great honour among the poets of the sixteenth century. "In three hundred and fifty years," says her biographer, Visconti, "there has been no other Italian lady who can be compared to her." "It is written with good taste, with quick and intelligent sympathy, occasionally with a real freshness and charm of style."—PALL MALL GAZETTE.

Volunteer's Scrap Book. By the Author of "The Cambridge Scrap Book." Crown 4to. 7s. 6d.

"A genial and clever caricaturist in whom we may often perceive through small details that he has as proper a sense of the graceful as of the ludicrous. The author might be and probably is a Volunteer himself, so kindly is the mirth he makes of all the incidents and phrases of the drill-ground."—EXAMINER.

Wandering Willie. By the Author of "Effie's Friends," and "John Hatherton." Third Edition. Crown 8vo. 6s.

"This is an idyll of rare truth and beauty. . . . The story is simple and touching, the style of extraordinary delicacy, precision, and picturesqueness. . . . A charming gift-book for young ladies not yet promoted to novels, and will amply repay those of their elders who may give an hour to its perusal."—DAILY NEWS.

Webster.—Works by AUGUSTA WEBSTER:—

"If Mrs. Webster only remains true to herself, she will assuredly take a higher rank as a poet than any woman has yet done."—WESTMINSTER REVIEW.

DRAMATIC STUDIES. Extra fcap. 8vo. 5s.

"A volume as strongly marked by perfect taste as by poetic power."—NONCONFORMIST.

A WOMAN SOLD, AND OTHER POEMS. Crown 8vo. 7s. 6d.

"Mrs. Webster has shown us that she is able to draw admirably from the life; that she can observe with subtlety, and render her observations with delicacy; that she can impersonate complex conceptions and venture into which few living writers can follow her."—GUARDIAN.

Webster—*continued.*

PORTRAITS. Second Edition. Extra fcap. 8vo. 3s. 6d.

"*Mrs. Webster's poems exhibit simplicity and tenderness . . . her taste is perfect . . . This simplicity is combined with a subtlety of thought, feeling, and observation which demand that attention which only real lovers of poetry are apt to bestow.*"—WESTMINSTER REVIEW.

PROMETHEUS BOUND OF ÆSCHYLUS. Literally translated into English Verse. Extra fcap. 8vo. 3s. 6d.

"*Closeness and simplicity combined with literary skill.*" — ATHENÆUM. "*Mrs. Webster's 'Dramatic Studies' and 'Translation of Prometheus' have won for her an honourable place among our female poets. She writes with remarkable vigour and dramatic realization, and bids fair to be the most successful claimant of Mrs. Browning's mantle.*"—BRITISH QUARTERLY REVIEW.

MEDEA OF EURIPIDES. Literally translated into English Verse. Extra fcap. 8vo. 3s. 6d.

"*Mrs. Webster's translation surpasses our utmost expectations. It is a photograph of the original without any of that harshness which so often accompanies a photograph.*"—WESTMINSTER REVIEW.

THE AUSPICIOUS DAY. A Dramatic Poem. Extra fcap. 8vo. 5s.

Westminster Plays. Lusus Alteri Westmonasterienses, Sive Prologi et Epilogi ad Fabulas in S^{ti} Petri Collegio : actas qui Exstabant collecti et justa quoad licuit annorum serie ordinati, quibus accedit Declamationum quæ vocantur et Epigrammatum Delectus. Curantibus J. MURE, A.M., H. BULL, A.M., C. B. SCOTT, B.D. 8vo. 12s. 6d.

IDEM.—Pars Secunda, 1820—1864. Quibus accedit Epigrammatum Delectus. 8vo. 15s.

When I was a Little Girl. STORIES FOR CHILDREN. By the Author of "St. Olave's." Third Edition. Extra fcap. 8vo. 4s. 6d. With Eight Illustrations by L. FRÖLICH.

"*At the head, and a long way ahead, of all books for girls, we* place 'When I was a Little Girl.'"—TIMES. "It is one of the choicest morsels of child-biography which we have met with."—NONCONFORMIST.

Wollaston.—LYRA DEVONIENSIS. By T. V. WOLLASTON, M.A. Fcap. 8vo. 3s. 6d.

"*It is the work of a man of refined taste, of deep religious sentiment, a true artist, and a good Christian.*"—CHURCH TIMES.

Woolner.—MY BEAUTIFUL LADY. By THOMAS WOOLNER. With a Vignette by ARTHUR HUGHES. Third Edition. Fcap. 8vo. 5s.

"*It is clearly the product of no idle hour, but a highly-conceived and faithfully-executed task, self-imposed, and prompted by that inward yearning to utter great thoughts, and a wealth of passionate feeling, which is poetic genius. No man can read this poem without being struck by the fitness and finish of the workmanship, so to speak, as well as by the chastened and unpretending loftiness of thought which pervades the whole.*"—GLOBE.

Words from the Poets. Selected by the Editor of "Rays of Sunlight." With a Vignette and Frontispiece. 18mo. limp., 1s.

"*The selection aims at popularity, and deserves it.*"—GUARDIAN.

Wyatt (Sir M. Digby).—FINE ART : a Sketch of its History, Theory, Practice, and application to Industry. A Course of Lectures delivered before the University of Cambridge. By Sir M. DIGBY WYATT, M.A. Slade Professor of Fine Art. 8vo. 10s. 6d.

"*An excellent handbook for the student of art.*"—GRAPHIC. "*The book abounds in valuable matter, and will therefore be read with pleasure and profit by lovers of art.*"—DAILY NEWS.

Yonge (C. M.)—Works by CHARLOTTE M. YONGE. (See also CATALOGUE OF WORKS IN HISTORY, and EDUCATIONAL CATALOGUE.)

THE HEIR OF REDCLYFFE. Eighteenth Edition. With Illustrations. Crown 8vo. 6s.

Yonge (C. M.)—*continued.*

HEARTSEASE. Eleventh Edition. With Illustrations. Crown 8vo. 6s.

THE DAISY CHAIN. Tenth Edition. With Illustrations. Crown 8vo. 6s.

THE TRIAL: MORE LINKS OF THE DAISY CHAIN. Fifth Edition. With Illustrations. Crown 8vo. 6s.

DYNEVOR TERRACE. Fourth Edition. Crown 8vo. 6s.

HOPES AND FEARS. Third Edition. Crown 8vo. 6s.

THE YOUNG STEPMOTHER. Third Edition. Crown 8vo. 6s.

CLEVER WOMAN OF THE FAMILY. Second Edition. Crown 8vo. 6s.

THE DOVE IN THE EAGLE'S NEST. Second Edition. Crown 8vo. 6s.

"*We think the authoress of 'The Heir of Redclyffe' has surpassed her previous efforts in this illuminated chronicle of the olden time.*"
—BRITISH QUARTERLY.

THE CAGED LION. Illustrated. Crown 8vo. 6s.

"*Prettily and tenderly written, and will with young people especially be a great favourite.*"—DAILY NEWS. "*Everybody should read this.*"—LITERARY CHURCHMAN.

THE CHAPLET OF PEARLS; OR, THE WHITE AND BLACK RIBAUMONT. Crown 8vo. 6s.

"*Miss Yonge has brought a lofty aim as well as high art to the construction of a story which may claim a place among the best efforts in historical romance.*"—MORNING POST. "*The plot, in truth, is of the very first order of merit.*"—SPECTATOR. "*We have seldom read a more charming story.*"—GUARDIAN.

THE PRINCE AND THE PAGE. A Tale of the Last Crusade. Illustrated. 18mo. 3s. 6d.

Yonge (C. M.)—*continued.*

"*A tale which, we are sure, will give pleasure to many others besides the young people for whom it is specially intended. ... This extremely prettily-told story does not require the guarantee afforded by the name of the author of 'The Heir of Redclyffe' on the title-page to ensure its becoming a universal favourite.*"—DUBLIN EVENING MAIL.

THE LANCES OF LYNWOOD. New Edition, with Coloured Illustrations. 18mo. 4s. 6d.

"*The illustrations are very spirited and rich in colour, and the story can hardly fail to charm the youthful reader.*"—MANCHESTER EXAMINER.

THE LITTLE DUKE: RICHARD THE FEARLESS. New Edition. Illustrated. 18mo. 3s. 6d.

A STOREHOUSE OF STORIES. First and Second Series. Globe 8vo. 3s. 6d. each.

CONTENTS OF FIRST SERIES:—History of Philip Quarll—Goody Twoshoes—The Governess—Jemima Placid—The Perambulations of a Mouse—The Village School—The Little Queen—History of Little Jack.

"*Miss Yonge has done great service to the infantry of this generation by putting these eleven stories of sage simplicity within their reach.*"—BRITISH QUARTERLY REVIEW.

CONTENTS OF SECOND SERIES:—Family Stories—Elements of Morality—A Puzzle for a Curious Girl—Blossoms of Morality.

A BOOK OF GOLDEN DEEDS OF ALL TIMES AND ALL COUNTRIES. Gathered and Narrated Anew. New Edition, with Twenty Illustrations by FRÖLICH. Crown 8vo. cloth gilt. 6s. (See also GOLDEN TREASURY SERIES). Cheap Edition. 1s.

"*We have seen no prettier gift-book for a long time, and none which, both for its cheapness and the spirit in which it has been compiled, is more deserving of praise.*"—ATHENÆUM.

A BOOK OF WORTHIES.—See GOLDEN TREASURY SERIES.

Yonge (C.M.)—*continued.*

LITTLE LUCY'S WONDERFUL GLOBE. Pictured by Frölich, and narrated by Charlotte M. Yonge. Second Edition. Crown 4to. cloth gilt. 6s.

Miss Yonge's wonderful "knack" of instructive story-telling to children is well known. In this volume, in a manner which cannot but prove interesting to all boys and girls, she manages to convey a wonderful amount of information concerning most of the countries of the world; in this she is considerably aided by the twenty-four telling pictures of Mr. Frölich. "'Lucy's Wonderful Globe' is capital, and will give its youthful readers more idea of foreign countries and customs than any number of books of geography or travel."—Graphic.

CAMEOS FROM ENGLISH HISTORY. From Rollo to Edward II. Extra fcap. 8vo. 5s. Second Edition, enlarged. 5s.

A Second Series. THE WARS IN FRANCE. Extra fcap. 8vo. 5s.

The endeavour has not been to chronicle facts, but to put together a series of pictures of persons and events, so as to arrest the attention, and give some individuality and distinctness to the recollection, by gathering together details at the most memorable moments. The "Cameos" are intended as a book for young people just beyond the elementary histories of England, and able to enter in some degree into the real spirit of events, and to be struck with characters and scenes presented in some relief. "Instead of dry details," says the Nonconformist, *"we have living pictures, faithful, vivid, and striking."*

Young.—MEMOIR OF CHARLES MAYNE YOUNG, Tragedian. With Extracts from his Son's Journal. By Julian Charles Young, M.A., Rector of Ilmington. New and Cheaper Edition. Crown 8vo. 7s. 6d. With Portraits and Sketches.

"There is hardly a page of it which was not worth printing. There is hardly a line which has not some kind of interest attaching

to it."—GUARDIAN. "*In this budget of anecdotes, fables, and gossip, old and new, relative to Scott, Moore, Chalmers, Coleridge, Wordsworth, Croker, Mathews, the Third and Fourth Georges, Bowles, Beckford, Lockhart, Wellington, Peel, Louis Napoleon, D'Orsay, Dickens, Thackeray, Louis Blanc, Gibson, Constable, and Stanfield (the list might be much extended), the reader must be hard indeed to please who cannot find entertainment.*"—PALL MALL GAZETTE.

MACMILLAN'S

GOLDEN TREASURY SERIES.

UNIFORMLY printed in 18mo., with Vignette Titles by Sir NOEL PATON, T. WOOLNER, W. HOLMAN HUNT, J. E. MILLAIS, ARTHUR HUGHES, &c. Engraved on Steel by JEENS. Bound in extra cloth, 4s. 6d. each volume. Also kept in morocco and calf bindings.

> "*Messrs. Macmillan have, in their Golden Treasury Series, especially provided editions of standard works, volumes of selected poetry, and original compositions, which entitle this series to be called classical. Nothing can be better than the literary execution, nothing more elegant than the material workmanship.*"—BRITISH QUARTERLY REVIEW.

The Golden Treasury of the Best Songs and LYRICAL POEMS IN THE ENGLISH LANGUAGE.
Selected and arranged, with Notes, by FRANCIS TURNER PALGRAVE.

> "*This delightful little volume, the Golden Treasury, which contains many of the best original lyrical pieces and songs in our language, grouped with care and skill, so as to illustrate each other like the pictures in a well-arranged gallery.*"—QUARTERLY REVIEW.

The Children's Garland from the best Poets.
Selected and arranged by COVENTRY PATMORE.

> "*It includes specimens of all the great masters in the art of poetry, selected with the matured judgment of a man concentrated on obtaining insight into the feelings and tastes of childhood, and*

D

desirous to awaken its finest impulses, to cultivate its keenest sensibilities."—MORNING POST.

The Book of Praise. From the Best English Hymn Writers. Selected and arranged by Sir ROUNDELL PALMER. *A New and Enlarged Edition.*

"*All previous compilations of this kind must undeniably for the present give place to the Book of Praise. . . . The selection has been made throughout with sound judgment and critical taste. The pains involved in this compilation must have been immense, embracing, as it does, every writer of note in this special province of English literature, and ranging over the most widely divergent tracks of religious thought.*"—SATURDAY REVIEW.

The Fairy Book; the Best Popular Fairy Stories. Selected and rendered anew by the Author of "JOHN HALIFAX, GENTLEMAN."

"*A delightful selection, in a delightful external form; full of the physical splendour and vast opulence of proper fairy tales.*"—SPECTATOR.

The Ballad Book. A Selection of the Choicest British Ballads. Edited by WILLIAM ALLINGHAM.

"*His taste as a judge of old poetry will be found, by all acquainted with the various readings of old English ballads, true enough to justify his undertaking so critical a task.*"—SATURDAY REVIEW.

The Jest Book. The Choicest Anecdotes and Sayings. Selected and arranged by MARK LEMON.

"*The fullest and best jest book that has yet appeared.*"—SATURDAY REVIEW.

Bacon's Essays and Colours of Good and Evil. With Notes and Glossarial Index. By W. ALDIS WRIGHT, M.A.

"*The beautiful little edition of Bacon's Essays, now before us, does credit to the taste and scholarship of Mr. Aldis Wright. . . . It puts the reader in possession of all the essential literary facts and chronology necessary for reading the Essays in connection with Bacon's life and times.*"—SPECTATOR. "*By far the most complete as well as the most elegant edition we possess.*"—WESTMINSTER REVIEW.

The Pilgrim's Progress from this World to that which is to come. By JOHN BUNYAN.

"*A beautiful and scholarly reprint.*"—SPECTATOR.

The Sunday Book of Poetry for the Young. Selected and arranged by C. F. ALEXANDER.

"*A well-selected volume of Sacred Poetry.*"—SPECTATOR.

A Book of Golden Deeds of All Times and All Countries. Gathered and narrated anew. By the Author of "THE HEIR OF REDCLYFFE."

"*... To the young, for whom it is especially intended, as a most interesting collection of thrilling tales well told; and to their elders, as a useful handbook of reference, and a pleasant one to take up when their wish is to while away a weary half-hour. We have seen no prettier gift-book for a long time.*"—ATHENÆUM.

The Poetical Works of Robert Burns. Edited, with Biographical Memoir, Notes, and Glossary, by ALEXANDER SMITH. Two Vols.

"*Beyond all question this is the most beautiful edition of Burns yet out.*"—EDINBURGH DAILY REVIEW.

The Adventures of Robinson Crusoe. Edited from the Original Edition by J. W. CLARK, M.A., Fellow of Trinity College, Cambridge.

"*Mutilated and modified editions of this English classic are so much the rule, that a cheap and pretty copy of it, rigidly exact to the original, will be a prize to many book-buyers.*"—EXAMINER.

The Republic of Plato. TRANSLATED into ENGLISH, with Notes by J. Ll. DAVIES, M.A. and D. J. VAUGHAN, M.A.

"*A dainty and cheap little edition.*"—EXAMINER.

The Song Book. Words and Tunes from the best Poets and Musicians. Selected and arranged by JOHN HULLAH, Professor of Vocal Music in King's College, London.

"*A choice collection of the sterling songs of England, Scotland, and Ireland, with the music of each prefixed to the words. How much true wholesome pleasure such a book can diffuse, and will diffuse, we trust, through many thousand families.*"—EXAMINER.

La Lyre Française. Selected and arranged, with Notes, by GUSTAVE MASSON, French Master in Harrow School.

A selection of the best French songs and lyrical pieces.

Tom Brown's School Days. By AN OLD BOY.

"*A perfect gem of a book. The best and most healthy book about boys for boys that ever was written.*"—ILLUSTRATED TIMES.

A Book of Worthies. Gathered from the Old Histories and written anew by the Author of "THE HEIR OF REDCLYFFE." With Vignette.

"*An admirable addition to an admirable series.*"—WESTMINSTER REVIEW.

A Book of Golden Thoughts. By HENRY ATTWELL, Knight of the Order of the Oak Crown.

"*Mr. Attwell has produced a book of rare value . . . . Happily it is small enough to be carried about in the pocket, and of such a companion it would be difficult to weary.*"—PALL MALL GAZETTE.

Guesses at Truth. By TWO BROTHERS. New Edition.

MACMILLAN'S

GLOBE LIBRARY.

Beautifully printed on toned paper and bound in cloth extra, gilt edges, price 4s. 6d. each; in cloth plain, 3s. 6d. Also kept in a variety of calf and morocco bindings at moderate prices.

BOOKS, Wordsworth says, are

"the spirit breathed
By dead men to their kind;"

and the aim of the publishers of the Globe Library has been to make it possible for the universal kin of English-speaking men to hold communion with the loftiest "spirits of the mighty dead;" to put within the reach of all classes *complete* and *accurate* editions, carefully and clearly printed upon the best paper, in a convenient form, at a moderate price, of the works of the MASTER-MINDS OF ENGLISH LITERATURE, and occasionally of foreign literature in an attractive English dress.

The Editors, by their scholarship and special study of their authors, are competent to afford every assistance to readers of all kinds: this assistance is rendered by original biographies, glossaries of unusual or obsolete words, and critical and explanatory notes.

The publishers hope, therefore, that these Globe Editions may prove worthy of acceptance by all classes wherever the English Language is spoken, and by their universal circulation justify their distinctive epithet; while at the same time they spread and nourish a common sympathy with nature's most "finely touched" spirits, and thus help a little to "make the whole world kin."

The SATURDAY REVIEW *says:* "*The Globe Editions are admirable for their scholarly editing, their typographical excellence, their compendious form, and their cheapness.*" *The* BRITISH QUARTERLY REVIEW *says:* "*In compendiousness, elegance, and scholarliness, the Globe Editions of Messrs. Macmillan surpass any popular series of our classics hitherto given to the public. As near an approach to miniature perfection as has ever been made.*"

Shakespeare's Complete Works. Edited by W. G. CLARK, M.A., and W. ALDIS WRIGHT, M.A., of Trinity College, Cambridge, Editors of the "Cambridge Shakespeare. With Glossary. pp. 1,075. Price 3s. 6d.

This edition aims at presenting a perfectly reliable text of the complete works of "the foremost man in all literature." The text is essentially the same as that of the "Cambridge Shakespeare." Appended is a Glossary containing the meaning of every word in the text which is either obsolete or is used in an antiquated or unusual sense. This, combined with the method used to indicate corrupted readings, serves to a great extent the purpose of notes. The ATHENÆUM *says this edition is "a marvel of beauty, cheapness, and compactness. ... For the busy man, above all for the working student, this is the best of all existing Shakespeares." And the* PALL MALL GAZETTE *observes:* "*To have produced the complete works of the world's greatest poet in such a form, and at a price within the reach of every one, is of itself almost sufficient to give the publishers a claim to be considered public benefactors.*"

Spenser's Complete Works. Edited from the Original Editions and Manuscripts, by R. MORRIS, with a Memoir by J. W. HALES, M.A. With Glossary. pp. lv., 736. Price 3s. 6d.

The text of the poems has been reprinted from the earliest known editions, carefully collated with subsequent ones, most of which were published in the poet's lifetime. Spenser's only prose work, his sagacious and interesting "View of the State of Ireland," has been re-edited from three manuscripts belonging to the British Museum. A complete Glossary and a list of all the most important various readings serve to a large extent the purpose of notes explanatory and critical. An exhaustive general Index and a useful "Index of first lines" precede the poems; and in an Appendix are given Spenser's Letters to Gabriel Harvey. "Worthy—and higher praise it needs not—of the beautiful 'Globe Series.' The work is edited with all the care so noble a poet deserves."—DAILY NEWS.

Sir Walter Scott's Poetical Works. Edited with a Biographical and Critical Memoir by FRANCIS TURNER PALGRAVE, and copious Notes. pp. xliii., 559. Price 3s. 6d.

"Scott," says Heine, "in his every book, gladdens, tranquillizes, and strengthens my heart." This edition contains the whole of Scott's poetical works, with the exception of one or two short poems. While most of Scott's own notes have been retained, others have been added explaining many historical and topographical allusions; and original introductions from the pen of a gentleman familiar with Scotch literature and scenery, containing much interesting information, antiquarian, historical, and biographical, are prefixed to the principal poems. "We can almost sympathise with a middle-aged grumbler, who, after reading Mr. Palgrave's memoir and introduction, should exclaim—'Why was there not such an edition of Scott when I was a schoolboy?'"—GUARDIAN.

Complete Works of Robert Burns.—THE POEMS, SONGS, AND LETTERS, edited from the best Printed and Manuscript Authorities, with Glossarial Index, Notes, and a Biographical Memoir by ALEXANDER SMITH. pp. lxii., 636. Price 3s. 6d.

Burns's poems and songs need not circulate exclusively among Scotchmen, but should be read by all who wish to know the multitudinous capabilities of the Scotch language, and who have the capacity of appreciating the exquisite expression of all kinds of human feeling—rich pawky humour, keen wit, withering satire, genuine pathos, pure passionate love. The exhaustive glossarial index and the copious notes will make all the purely Scotch poems intelligible even to an Englishman. Burns's letters must be read by all who desire fully to appreciate the poet's character, to see it on all its many sides. Explanatory notes are prefixed to most of these letters, and Burns's Journals kept during his Border and Highland Tours, are appended. Following the prefixed biography by the editor, is a Chronological Table of Burns's Life and Works. "Admirable in all respects."—SPECTATOR. *"The cheapest, the most perfect, and the most interesting edition which has ever been published."*—BELL'S MESSENGER.

Robinson Crusoe. Edited after the Original Editions, with a Biographical Introduction by HENRY KINGSLEY. pp. xxxi., 607. Price 3s. 6d.

Of this matchless truth-like story, it is scarcely possible to find an unabridged edition. This edition may be relied upon as containing the whole of "Robinson Crusoe" as it came from the pen of its author, without mutilation, and with all peculiarities religiously preserved. These points, combined with its handsome paper, large clear type, and moderate price, ought to render this par excellence *the "Globe," the Universal edition of Defoe's fascinating narrative. "A most excellent and in every way desirable edition."*—COURT CIRCULAR. *"Macmillan's 'Globe' Robinson Crusoe is a book to have and to keep."*—MORNING STAR.

Goldsmith's Miscellaneous Works. Edited, with Biographical Introduction, by Professor MASSON. pp. lx., 695. Globe 8vo. 3s. 6d.

This volume comprehends the whole of the prose and poetical works of this most genial of English authors, those only being excluded which are mere compilations. They are all accurately reprinted from the most reliable editions. The faithfulness, fulness, and literary merit of the biography are sufficiently attested by the name of its author, Professor Masson. It contains many interesting anecdotes which will give the reader an insight into Goldsmith's character, and many graphic pictures of the literary life of London during the middle of last century. "Such an admirable compendium of the facts of Goldsmith's life, and so careful and minute a delineation of the mixed traits of his peculiar character as to be a very model of a literary biography in little."—SCOTSMAN.

Pope's Poetical Works. Edited, with Notes and Introductory Memoir, by ADOLPHUS WILLIAM WARD, M.A., Fellow of St. Peter's College, Cambridge, and Professor of History in Owens College, Manchester. pp. lii., 508. Globe 8vo. 3s. 6d.

> This edition contains all Pope's poems, translations, and adaptations, —his now superseded Homeric translations alone being omitted. The text, carefully revised, is taken from the best editions; Pope's own use of capital letters and apostrophised syllables, frequently necessary to an understanding of his meaning, has been preserved; while his uncertain spelling and his frequently perplexing interpunctuation have been judiciously amended. Abundant notes are added, including Pope's own, the best of those of previous editors, and many which are the result of the study and research of the present editor. The introductory Memoir will be found to shed considerable light on the political, social, and literary life of the period in which Pope filled so large a space. The LITERARY CHURCHMAN remarks: "The editor's own notes and introductory memoir are excellent, the memoir alone would be cheap and well worth buying at the price of the whole volume."

Dryden's Poetical Works. Edited, with a Memoir, Revised Text, and Notes, by W. D. CHRISTIE, M.A., of Trinity College, Cambridge. pp. lxxxvii., 662. Globe 8vo. 3s. 6d.

> A study of Dryden's works is absolutely necessary to anyone who wishes to understand thoroughly, not only the literature, but also the political and religious history of the eventful period when he lived and reigned as literary dictator. In this edition of his works, which comprises several specimens of his vigorous prose, the text has been thoroughly corrected and purified from many misprints and small changes often materially affecting the sense, which had been allowed to slip in by previous editors. The old spelling has been retained where it is not altogether strange or repulsive. Besides an exhaustive Glossary, there are copious Notes, critical, historical, biographical, and explanatory; and the biography contains the results of considerable original research, which has served to shed light on several hitherto obscure circumstances connected with the life and parentage of the poet. "An admirable edition, the result of great research and of a careful revision of the text. The memoir prefixed contains, within less than ninety pages, as much sound criticism and as comprehensive a biography as the student of Dryden need desire."—PALL MALL GAZETTE.

Cowper's Poetical Works. Edited, with Notes and Biographical Introduction, by WILLIAM BENHAM, Vicar of Addington and Professor of Modern History in Queen's College, London. pp. lxxiii., 536. Globe 8vo. 3s. 6d.

> This volume contains, arranged under seven heads, the whole of Cowper's own poems, including several never before published, and all his translations except that of Homer's "Iliad." The text is taken from the original editions, and Cowper's own notes are given at the foot of the page, while many explanatory notes by the editor himself are appended to the volume. In the very full Memoir it will be found that much new light has been thrown on some of the most difficult passages of Cowper's spiritually chequered life. "Mr. Benham's edition of Cowper is one of permanent value. The biographical introduction is excellent, full of information, singularly neat and readable and modest—indeed too modest in its comments. The notes are concise and accurate, and the editor has been able to discover and introduce some hitherto unprinted matter. Altogether the book is a very excellent one."—SATURDAY REVIEW.

Morte d'Arthur.—SIR THOMAS MALORY'S BOOK OF KING ARTHUR AND OF HIS NOBLE KNIGHTS OF THE ROUND TABLE. The original Edition of CAXTON, revised for Modern Use. With an Introduction by Sir EDWARD STRACHEY, Bart. pp. xxxvii., 509. Globe 8vo. 3s. 6d.

> This volume contains the cream of the legends of chivalry which have gathered round the shadowy King Arthur and his Knights of the Round Table. Tennyson has drawn largely on them in his cycle of Arthurian Idylls. The language is simple and quaint as that of the Bible, and the many stories of knightly adventure of which the book is made up, are fascinating as those of the "Arabian Nights." The great moral of the book is to "do after the good, and leave the evil." There was a want of an edition of the work at a moderate price, suitable for ordinary readers, and especially for boys: such an edition the present professes to be. The Introduction contains an account of the Origin and Matter of the book, the Text and its several Editions, and an Essay on Chivalry, tracing its history from its origin to its decay. Notes are appended, and a

Glossary of such words as require explanation. "It is with perfect confidence that we recommend this edition of the old romance to every class of readers."—PALL MALL GAZETTE.

The Works of Virgil. Rendered into English Prose, with Introductions, Notes, Running Analysis, and an Index. By JAMES LONSDALE, M.A., late Fellow and Tutor of Balliol College, Oxford, and Classical Professor in King's College, London; and SAMUEL LEE, M.A., Latin Lecturer at University College, London. pp. 288. Price 3s. 6d.

> The publishers believe that an accurate and readable translation of all the works of Virgil is perfectly in accordance with the object of the "Globe Library." A new prose-translation has therefore been made by two competent scholars, who have rendered the original faithfully into simple Bible-English, without paraphrase; and at the same time endeavoured to maintain as far as possible the rhythm and majestic flow of the original. On this latter point the DAILY TELEGRAPH says, "The endeavour to preserve in some degree a rhythm in the prose rendering is almost invariably successful and pleasing in its effect;" and the EDUCATIONAL TIMES, that it "may be readily recommended as a model for young students for rendering the poet into English." The General Introduction will be found full of interesting information as to the life of Virgil, the history of opinion concerning his writings, the notions entertained of him during the Middle Ages, editions of his works, his influence on modern poets and on education. To each of his works is prefixed a critical and explanatory introduction, and important aid is afforded to the thorough comprehension of each production by the running Analysis. Appended is an Index of all the proper names and the most important subjects occurring throughout the poems and introductions. "A more complete edition of Virgil in English it is scarcely possible to conceive than the scholarly work before us." —GLOBE.

www.ingramcontent.com/pod-product-compliance
Lightning Source LLC
Chambersburg PA
CBHW021352230426
43666CB00006B/496